RESPECT

*This book is dedicated
to the wonderful teaching team at
Childspace Early Learning Centres
~ past, present & future*

A practitioner's guide to calm & nurturing infant care & education

Toni Christie

with photographs by Bridget McBride

Copyright © 2011 Childspace Early Childhood Institute
Printed in Wellington, New Zealand
Published by:

Every effort has been made to locate copyright and permission information.

foreword

If you already know something about Pikler, Gerber, and RIE, you are going to love this book! If you never heard of Emmi Pikler or Magda Gerber and the organisation called RIE, you're in for a nice surprise. Toni Christie has done an admirable job of explaining some important concepts that can be used in infant-toddler early care and education programmes, concepts that all fall in the category called being respectful. She not only explains, she also shows, throughout the book, what it means to be respectful as she describes the behaviours that go with the attitude.

Toni provides a thorough discussion and illustrations of primary caregiving and how it is a way of building trusting relationships – an important aspect of infant-toddler care. Toni defines the term, tells how to do it, and she also explains the kinds of misconceptions some people have about primary care. Woven through the primary care chapter and the other chapters as well is the theme of observation – what Toni calls, "peaceful observation." It's a way to get to know each baby and understand what each needs.

Perhaps the most unusual feature of the approach Toni is advocating in this book is what is called freedom of movement. The theory originated with Dr. Emmi Pikler, from Budapest, Hungary and was carried to the United States of America by Magda Gerber, her friend and colleague. If you don't know about the advantages of allowing babies to move freely, read on. Toni has some compelling statements about how and why it works. She not only explains the concepts but also shows them in action.

It's tempting when writing a book like this to try to sell the readers on the approach – to try to convince them that it's the "right way" to care for infants and toddlers. Toni goes a step further. She looks at what she is advocating as a "good way" but is also clear about cultural differences. I was pleased to see that she advocates including respect for parents and their ideas. And she illustrates how this works in the particular centre that she studied. She obviously fully understands the realities of infant-toddler care.

This book makes an important contribution to the literature of early care and education that focuses on infants and toddlers.

Janet Gonzalez-Mena, March 2011.

From the author
This book is based on the findings from my masterate thesis: *Practising with respect: What does that mean for teachers working with infants?* After all the work that goes into researching, analysing, and writing a thesis, I decided mine should be useful beyond the realms of academia. I have added illustrations and seriously condensed the word count to provide a synopsis of my findings and practical guidelines for teachers. I firmly believe that valuable information should be offered in a well presented, readable and user-friendly manner to enable the best dissemination of ideas. I wrote this book for practitioners working with infants in early childhood settings and I sincerely hope you will find it useful in your daily work and play with our very youngest citizens.

About the author
Toni Christie has a Master's Degree in Education and is the Director of Childspace Early Childhood Institute. Toni began her career as an early childhood teacher and maintains that early childhood is the most significant stage of every person's development. Currently Toni's work involves teaching adults about the importance of the early years.

Toni is married to her partner in business and life, Robin, and they share two wonderful children, Tui and Max. Toni and Robin have written books and resources, they edit and publish a quarterly magazine, design and build early childhood environments, and organise and host annual conferences for early childhood teachers. They are driven to provide practical, relevant, natural and aesthetic resources and environments for all who play and work with very young children. They love their jobs!

About the photographer
Bridget McBride has a Bachelor's Degree in Education and has been working with infants and toddlers since 2003. Her work with infants and toddlers has been strongly influenced by the ideas of Emmi Pikler and Magda Gerber. Bridget has completed four weeks of training with the Pikler Institute in Budapest to further her knowledge in this area. This has reinforced her belief in the way that she works with the children in her care. In 2007 Bridget was lucky enough to be part of the Centre of Innovation project that involved researching and reflecting on the way we work with respect and peacefulness in our care and education of infants and toddlers. Young children continue to amaze and delight Bridget every day, which has made it easy to combine her love for photography with her work.

Acknowledgements

Thanks to my research supervisors at Victoria University of Wellington and the whole team at Childspace where I undertook my research, particularly the two nursery teachers who so generously allowed me to observe their interactions with infants and toddlers. Your passion, commitment and skill in your work and play with the babies are an absolute inspiration and example to everyone in the field of early childhood education.

Life has been brought to these pages by the images of many beautiful babies and the wonderful teachers who care for them. Thank-you all for recognising the great value of sharing these special moments, and thank-you Bridget for capturing them so beautifully.

Norah Fryer, Anne Meade, Pennie Brownlee, Laura Briley and Janet Gonzalez-Mena were interested in my thesis and offered me valuable advice and input. Thank-you Norah and Pennie, for always encouraging me to think for myself and for stimulating my thinking with interesting questions! Thank-you Janet and Laura, the history you provided on the Pikler approach and the RIE philosophy, as well as the differences between the two, was invaluable and helped deliver a rich background on the origins of my subject. Anne, you give your time and expertise so generously, and the early childhood profession in Aotearoa and abroad has benefited greatly from your warmth and wisdom.

My sincere thanks are due to Natasha Kibble who introduced our organisation to the Pikler approach and RIE philosophy and to all the teachers at Childspace who have collectively developed a new understanding of what it is to think and act respectfully.

To my friends and colleagues at our home office who put up with me spending too much time on my study and not enough time on my work. You picked up my slack like the true professionals you are and managed to keep a very complex organisation running smoothly in the absence of its Director on many occasions throughout this process. I am forever grateful that I get to work with such a thoughtful, committed, hard-working and fun team.

Most importantly I thank my beautiful family, Robin, Max and Tui. The three of you have always accepted and supported my ambitions and crazy ideas. I love you most dearly and you will always be the most important people in my world.

contents

Chapter 1: **Introduction**	1

Chapter 2: **The Pikler approach & RIE philosophy**	7

Chapter 3: **Primary caregiving**	11
– Towards a definition	11
– What does the literature say?	11
– A team approach	15
– Body language, cues and gestures	19
– Language as invitation and explanation	19
– Close proximity of caregivers	20
– Unhurried time	21
– Wait for a turn	22
– Chapter summary	24
– Practical guidelines for implementation	27

Chapter 4: **Freedom of movement**	28
– Towards a definition	28
– What does the literature say?	29
– Teacher and parent definitions and views	35
– Teachers support and intervene only when necessary	39
– Teachers 'over-ride' the rules respectfully	40
– Peaceful observation	44
– Adoption versus adaptation of a philosophy	47
– Chapter summary	50

Chapter 5: **Respect**	51
– Towards a definition	51
– What does the literature say?	51
– Ethics of care	57
– Teachers invite children to engage	59

- Unhurried time 62
- Choices are offered 65
- Peaceful observation 67
- Teachers support rather than intervene 69
- A team approach is an important element 74
- Chapter summary 76
- Practical guidelines for implementation 79

Chapter 6: **Conclusion & recommendations** 80

- Primary caregiving 80
- Free movement 81
- Future research 83
- Respect 83
- Implications and recommendations for policy makers 84
- Practical recommendations for teachers 85

References & further reading 90

Publications available from Childspace Early Childhood Institute 94

chapter 1

Introduction

Once upon a time, for my master's thesis, I undertook a qualitative case study examining the teaching practices, inspired by the Pikler approach and Resources for Infant Educarers (RIE) philosophy, at a Childspace infant and toddler centre. The specific practices observed involved primary caregiving, freedom of movement and respect for infants' confidence and competence. The overall aim of the study was to explore these practices for the benefit of other practitioners wanting to emulate a similar environment. I have based this book on the findings from my research and sincerely hope it will be of practical use to teachers working with infants.

Respect, defined as *treating with consideration*, was the overarching feature underpinning the values and actions of teachers. Teachers engaged in ways that would suggest they accept each person as an individual with rights and freedoms. Teachers invited children to engage with them, and no action would be initiated for or with a child without his or her agreement. This agreement was shown through cues and gestures, to which the teachers were all highly attuned. Teachers slowed their pace intentionally and offered children choices in their care and education.

Peaceful observation from teachers enhanced their ability to interpret individual children's needs and wants and they would provide support for children rather than intervene unnecessarily.

In the following paragraphs I have defined the terms *primary caregiving, freedom of movement,* and *respect for infants' confidence and competence* in order to clarify for readers the meaning of these terms.

Primary caregiving can be defined as a way of working in an early childhood setting in which each team member is focused on enabling and supporting close attachments between individual children and individual teachers (Elfer, Goldschmied, & Selleck, 2003). Each teacher has responsibility for establishing and maintaining close reciprocal relationships with a small group of children and their families. A team approach to primary caregiving ensures there are also secondary caregivers and close relationships formed between all teachers and children present.

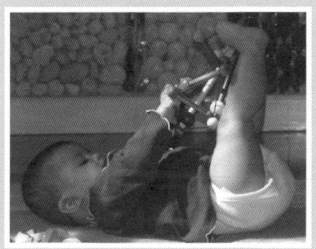

Freedom of movement can be described as *never putting a baby into a position she cannot get into or out of all by herself* (Gerber, 2002). This includes the elimination of all movement restricting devices such as belted swings, bouncinettes, and highchairs from the environment. Freedom of movement also means unassisted motor development. For instance, infants are placed on their backs until they can roll over on their own. They are not propped to sit or pulled up to stand via adult intervention.

Respect for infants' confidence and competence means considering them to be equal human beings, capable of problem solving and decision making. Viewing the child as capable means allowing them time and space and trusting them to develop and explore without unnecessary intervention.

In this book I have examined the actual practices involved in an infant curriculum based on primary caregiving and respect. I have explored the practices of free movement and discussed the value of adapting the RIE philosophy and Pikler approach and their relevance for early childhood settings in New Zealand. Finally, I have examined the term 'respect' and developed recommendations for respectful practice (see Chapter 6).

Photographs have been used to illustrate this book. In accordance with research ethics these images are not photographs of the actual children or teachers used in the process of my research. They are, however, useful in depicting the ideas about which I have written.

Tui

Where I have referred to direct observations and/or interview data from my research I have used pseudonyms so as not to identify any of the research participants. The two teachers and centre manager involved in the research are identified as pseudonyms of native New Zealand birds (Tui, Kea and Huia). Direct quotes from teachers are identified in speech bubbles attached to bird silhouettes. When I have referred to individual infants as an example as opposed to a direct observation I have tried to share between he and she pronouns for gender balance.

Kea

Huia

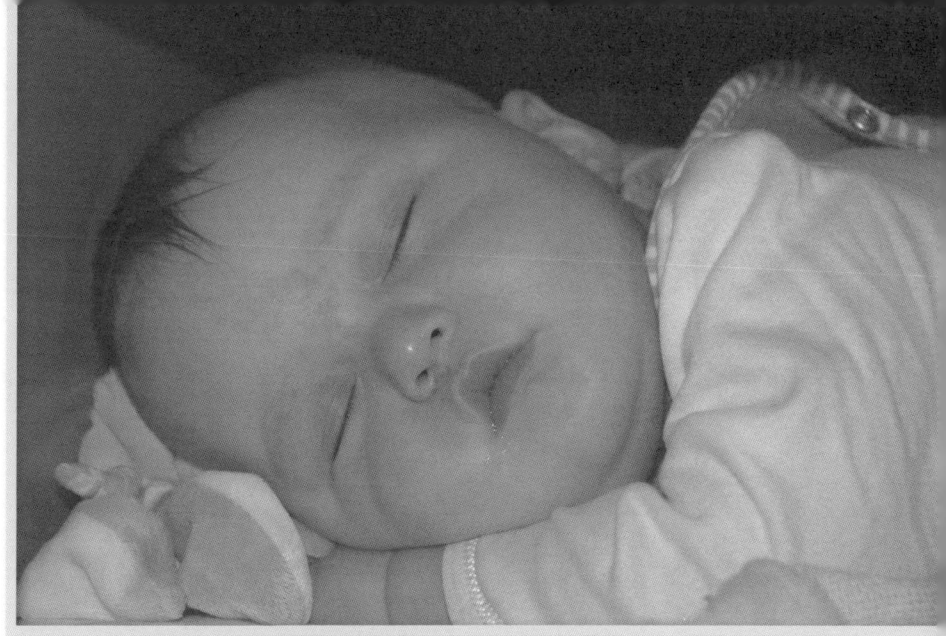

Infants need to be cared for with deep respect by people who understand the unique development and learning occurring for each child at this age. Infants and toddlers have no choice about where they are cared for, who cares for them, and myriad other aspects of their daily life. As adults it is important to acknowledge this fact and act responsibly in the best interests of the youngest and most vulnerable members of society.

Dr Emmi Pikler

chapter 2

The Pikler approach & RIE philosophy

The Pikler Institute is a residential nursery founded by Dr Emmi Pikler in 1946 in Budapest, Hungary. It was originally named the National Methodological Institute for Infant Care and Education and often referred to as 'Loczy' (pronounced 'Lote-zee'), after the street on which it is located. It originated after World War II when the Hungarian government asked Pikler to open a residential nursery (orphanage) for children under three years old whose families could not care for them. Pikler was a pioneer in the care and education of infants and toddlers long before the residential nursery opened. Dr Emmi Pikler was a paediatrician working with families in the 1930's and her theories originated through her work with infants and parents. She advocated for infants to be given our highest respect, focusing on the establishment of authentic trusting relationships between adult and infant. Her peaceful approach urges early childhood practitioners to consider infants and toddlers as competent, confident and unique individuals who are focused, self-initiating, involved,

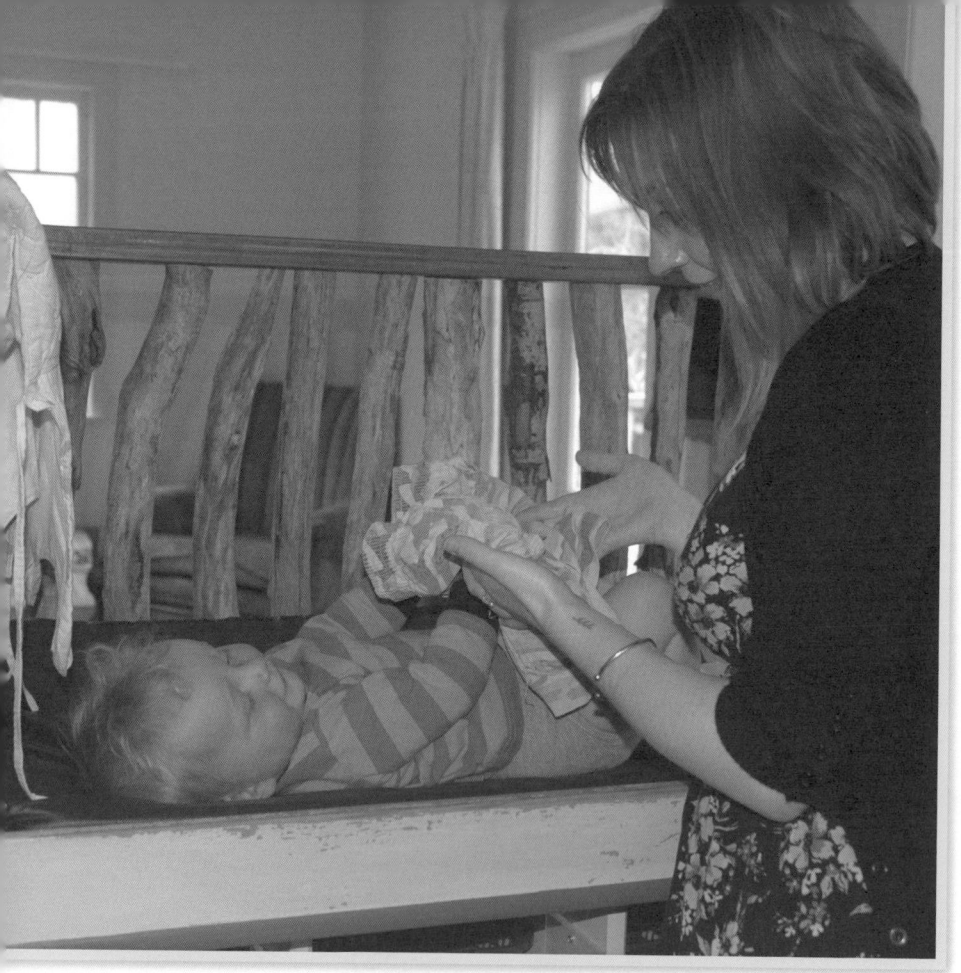

resourceful, secure, cooperative and curious (Gerber, 1984). She uses the descriptor 'peaceful' because she believes we need to create a safe, quiet environment, to slow down, pay attention and allow infants to move and play in their own way. Pikler was a dedicated researcher and kept meticulous records over many years detailing the normal development of infants at Loczy. Unfortunately because this work was conducted in communist-era Hungary, when communication with the West was extremely limited, only recently have Pikler's findings been translated into English (Association Pikler-Loczy, 2005; Sensory Awareness Foundation, 1994). When Emmi Pikler died in 1984 the institute she started and ran dedicatedly for some thirty-eight years was renamed the Emmi Pikler National Methodological Institute for Residential Nurseries. It is often referred to now as simply "The Pikler Institute".

As a mother, Magda Gerber first met Pikler when she was a paediatrician. Gerber was so intrigued and impressed by the respectful way Pikler spoke to Gerber's child, she became interested in Pikler's approach and subsequently worked alongside her at Loczy. Magda Gerber was able to pioneer Dr. Emmi Pikler's work in the United States, when she emigrated there from Hungary. The Resources for Infant Educarers (RIE) Institute is located in California, and was founded in 1978. RIE is a non-profit membership organisation concerned with improving the care and education of infants (Gerber, 2002).

Both Pikler and Gerber suggest we demonstrate our respect every time we interact with infants. Respect to these pioneers meant treating an infant as a unique human being with problem-solving and decision making power and ability, not as an object (Gerber, 2002).

Because the ideas and practices are similar, the Pikler approach and RIE philosophy are often grouped together as though they are one philosophy. For example, the RIE/Pikler philosophy is defined as a respectful interactive approach to infant and toddler care and development through responsive and reciprocal relationships (Kovach & Da Ros, 1998; David & Appell, 2001). Respect is the basis of Dr Emmi Pikler's approach and Magda Gerber's RIE philosophy but there are some differences between the two.

One difference is obviously in the words *approach* versus *philosophy*. The word approach was chosen carefully by Anna Tardos, Pikler's daughter, who did not want Pikler's ideas rigidly defined as a methodology. Gerber was the one who used the term philosophy (J. Gonzalez-Mena, personal communication, August, 2010). Another difference between the two was that Pikler was a dedicated researcher while Gerber used to say that research can prove anything one wants to prove and, for whatever reason, her philosophy was never researched (J. Gonzalez-Mena, personal communication, August 2010).

The final and most fundamental difference between Pikler's approach and Gerber's RIE philosophy is that after 1946, Pikler worked predominantly with institutionalised children (orphans) in Hungary, and Gerber worked with families in Los Angeles teaching a parenting philosophy. Pikler caregivers were trained to create a special kind of attachment so that separation was not devastating to either caregiver or baby when the children leave to be adopted or move on to somewhere else (J. Gonzalez-Mena, personal communication, August 2010). Paradoxically, the RIE philosophy, borrowing heavily from the tenets of the Pikler approach, was taught as a parenting philosophy to promote parent-infant attachment. Essentially, Pikler's approach at the residential nursery, was dedicated to helping disadvantaged (orphaned) children to develop normally, and the RIE philosophy is dedicated to supporting parents in their role with infants.

For further background & information on the Pikler approach or RIE philosophy
www.pikler.org or www.rie.org

chapter 3

Primary caregiving

Towards a definition

Adopting a primary caregiving system in an early childhood setting essentially means that one teacher takes a lead role in caring for a small group of children. For the children this means someone with whom they can build a close and trusting relationship. It also means someone who will be there for them and respond to their needs and care for them. For the parents and whānau it means someone they will get to know well and with whom they will feel comfortable leaving their child. The primary caregiver is someone with whom both parents and child can build a close and trusting relationship.

What does the literature say?

In New Zealand, research regarding primary caregiving for infants has only recently emerged (Dalli, 2000; Rockel, 2002; Kibble, Cairns-Cowan, McBride, Corrigan, & Dalli, 2009, 2010; Dalli & Kibble, 2010; Christie, 2010). The term primary care is used to explain the responsive relationship between an infant and the most significant adult in their life, usually their mother (Bernhardt, 2000). It can also be used to describe an approach where a whole centre is focused on enabling and supporting close

reciprocal relationships between small groups of children and individual teachers or caregivers. Primary caregiving should not be confused as taking over the important primary care role of a parent, and for that reason some researchers investigating primary caregiving approaches have labeled it "the key person approach" (Elfer, Goldschmied & Selleck, 2003, p.18). Primary caregiving, or the key person approach, is a central tenet of the Pikler approach and the RIE philosophy and is a cornerstone of the philosophy at the case study centre. There is an understanding that valuable learning is taking place for the infant in the crucial routine care times in which they are engaged with one sensitive and responsive adult (Elfer, Goldschmied & Selleck, 2003; Gonzalez-Mena 2007; Dalli, 2000; Rockel, 2002; Kibble, Cairns-Cowan, McBride, Corrigan, & Dalli, 2009, 2010; Dalli & Kibble, 2010; Christie, 2010).

Gonzalez-Mena (2007) uses the term *caregiving as curriculum*, discussing the importance of adults being 'fully present' during individual care times with infants. *Caregiving as curriculum* refers to the idea that essential learning is taking place during these routine care times. Being fully present means paying full attention to the child during those care times and not being distracted by any other demands or happenings within the environment. The adult should not feel pressure to split his or her attention between the child being cared for and other responsibilities (Hammond, 2009). David and Appell (2001) suggest Pikler's approach includes an overall plan to help each child feel individually respected and secure in a close relationship with one special caregiver. These routine times where a relationship is strengthened through one-to-one uninterrupted interaction are sometimes referred to as *wants something* times (Gerber, 2002) or *prime times* (Greenman & Stonehouse, 1997).

Several researchers have identified the *prime times* or routine times such as feeding, changing and sleeping as when children and their primary caregiver are engaged together (Greenman & Stonehouse, 1997; Hutchins & Sims, 1999; Theilheimer, 2006). These *prime times* offer opportunities for adult/child interactions during intimate care moments. When these interactions are supported by team members who can help ensure the teacher and child have uninterrupted time together, opportunities are created for the development of trusting and secure relationships between adults and children.

> *Whenever you care, do it absolutely with full attention. If you pay half attention all the time, that's never full attention. Babies are then always half hungry for attention. But if you pay full attention part of the time, then you go a long way. That's what I would recommend: To be fully with a child and then let him be.* (Gerber, 2002, p. 7).

Te Whāriki (the New Zealand Early Childhood curriculum) clearly states that an infant's ability to thrive and learn is reliant on the establishment of a reciprocal, intimate, responsive and trusting relationship "with at least one other person within each setting" (Ministry of Education, 1996, p. 22). Recent neurological research regarding the influence of early childhood experiences on the developing brain suggest the role of primary caregiver is crucial with infants and toddlers when they are cared for outside the home (Shonkoff & Phillips, 2000).

There is support for primary caregiving in the literature (Theilheimer, 2006; Rockel, 2002: Bary, Deans, Charlton, Hullett, Martin, Martin, Moana, Waugh, Jordan, & Scrivens, 2009; Hammond, 2009; Elfer, Goldschmied & Selleck, 2003), but this does not always accurately reflect the practices in early childhood settings (Rockel, 2002).

In her master's thesis, Rockel found that primary caregiving is not widely practiced because of the view that it is exclusive and therefore difficult to make work in a setting where the primary caregiver will not always be available to the child. Elfer and colleagues (2003) list many reasons practitioners might be against a primary caregiving or key person approach such as: It brings staff too close to a parental role and they risk becoming over-involved; If children get too close to any one member of staff, it is painful for them if that member of staff is not available; It can be threatening for parents who may be jealous of a special relationship between their child and another adult; The key person approach is complex to organise and staff need to work as a team, not as individuals; It undermines the opportunities for children to participate in all nursery community relationships (Elfer, Goldschmied & Selleck, 2003, pp. 8 & 9).

Most of these reasons insinuate that primary caregiving is an individual approach as opposed to a team approach or that it is something understood by teachers and not by parents. As already noted, more recent research has found that primary caregiving is indeed a team effort, needs to be fully supported by a secondary caregiving system (Bary et al, 2009) and is in no way a form of replacement for the parent (Kibble et al, 2009; Christie, 2010).

The literature reviewed supports the implementation of a primary caregiving system. Strong arguments against the use of primary caregiving are based on perceptions as opposed to empirical evidence (Elfer, Goldschmied, & Selleck, 2003; Rockel, 2002).

A team approach

Recent Centres of Innovation (COI) research in New Zealand (Dalli & Kibble, 2010) considered primary caregiving within a given centre to have been enacted as a team approach and found that all teachers in the environment had a good understanding and relationship with each child in the environment. My findings support this research. Communication between teachers was respectful, clear and unhurried. Teachers shared information about children's needs and development. This collegial team approach was evident throughout the centre, not exclusively between the infant teachers.

Analysis of the observations showed that all teachers and support staff had a good knowledge of each individual child but the primary caregiver was usually the most knowledgeable and was therefore consulted or directly responsible for most decisions concerning the child or engagement in routine care times. On several occasions I observed teachers soothing a child anticipating the return of their primary caregiver to give them a meal or take them for a nappy change or sleep when they became available. I observed the primary caregiver taking responsibility for one-to-one care routine times whenever possible to ensure consistency and continuity for each child. I also observed children who were comfortable with a secondary or subsequent caregiver engaging with them at care times when necessary.

I observed teachers gathering necessary resources for each other. For example one teacher would heat a bottle for another teacher or warm a facecloth so the teacher engaged in caregiving could have uninterrupted time with the child, fully concentrating on him or her.

The teachers were careful to ensure they had all the correct details if they were coming back into the room after a break or just beginning a shift. They clarified this for me in the interviews.

It is only respectful to have a full picture of what is happening before launching in without the facts. (Huia: teacher interview).

Teachers were clear in their interviews about primary care being a whole team commitment.

Because they have the attachment with me but will build that up over time with the other teachers in the room (Kea: teacher interview).

If one is away the other becomes the primary caregiver to all and the regular reliever is still known but has to do what fits in with the children's wants. For example if they are not happy to be fed/changed etc by the reliever then the other caregiver does this (Kea: teacher interview).

Analysis of the data lead me to conclude that having a primary caregiving system in the case study centre required a full commitment from each member of the team. Everyone had to be clear about the value of primary caregiving and supportive of each other to ensure children were able to have uninterrupted care times with their primary caregiver whenever possible. There was also general acceptance of the fact that children would be consulted (by way of teachers being sensitive to their cues and gestures) regarding their desire or otherwise to be cared for by anyone other than their primary caregiver.

Body language, cues and gestures

Through sensitive observation teachers were able to accurately read infants' body language, cues and gestures. On many occasions I observed open hands held out with palms facing upwards by way of invitation from teachers in the environment. Acceptance of this invitation was usually indicated by the infant tipping his or her body forward towards the teacher.

I also observed similar examples of the invitation and acceptance sequence of cues working in the reverse order. Most often this involved children gesturing with open arms as a request or invitation for the caregiver to pick them up or cuddle them. Other examples of cues and gestures involved teachers reading the facial expressions and movements of children attempting to indicate their needs and wants. It is essential that caregivers are able to read the cues and gestures of pre-verbal infants as these are their primary form of communication.

For babies to thrive and be content, caregivers must accurately read their cues. When babies have the opportunity to express their needs and preferences, their well-being is recognised and maintained (Kovach and Da Ros-Voseles, 2008, p. 45).

Language as invitation and explanation

During the observations teachers were careful to explain to infants what they were doing and why. As previously stated, this is a matter of common courtesy for an infant who is otherwise unaware of what might be happening next. If we believe children should be the initiators of activity concerning their own well-being, then the teacher may be the one who asks or initiates the interaction, but it is through the cues and gestures of the child that their assent is gauged. Teachers used language to initiate activity with the child and they also used language to explain for a child what they might be feeling or what they might need. This is an essential skill for teachers working with infants as the infants are unable to communicate verbally through language and rely on the interpretation of sensitive caregivers to label their emotions and verbalise their desires.

Close proximity of caregivers

Refuelling (Petrie & Owen, 2005) is a common term used in connection with attachment and it refers to the repeated returns that a child makes to an attachment figure for emotional reassurance and comfort while they are exploring their environment.

The close proximity of their primary caregiver is often enough to soothe a distressed infant. Sometimes this is referred to in the literature as providing a *secure base* (Petrie & Owen, 2005, p. 144). Providing a *secure base* is similar to the idea of *refuelling* in that *refuelling* is initiated by the child as they touch base with the caregiver like a touch stone, giving them the courage to continue exploring independently. Providing a *secure base* refers to the role of the caregiver in offering closeness and reassurance to the infant while they independently explore. Teachers were comfortable to be nearby but were also comfortable not intervening and thereby encouraging children to solve their own problems as much as possible.

Unhurried time

[The adult is] emotionally available during caregiving times... [adults focus is] based on the emotional richness of an experience, not the length of time (Kovach and Da Ros-Voseles, 2008, p. 85).

The following example provides a rich illustration of the unhurried process teachers and children worked through together. Teachers were often just waiting for a response, avoiding rushing the child into moving faster than they desired.

> Tui asks Liv if she would like her nappy changed and I video the process. The change table is surrounded on three sides by dowel handrails in case the children prefer to be changed standing up. Liv is happy to lie down, and before she does she selects her nappy out of her locker and Tui gives Liv some cream to hold onto. Tui explains every part of the process to Liv as she is changing her, telling Liv when, how and why she is going to move her body. At one point she asks Liv if she can please move her leg down and Liv immediately obliges. Tui moves slowly and wipes Liv's bottom with two warm cloths telling her when she is going to use them and explaining: "Once more just so we get all the poos off your bottom." When Tui asks "Can I please have the cream now?" she holds out her hand and Liv places the cream into her hand. Tui moves slowly and explains everything as she is doing it. Before long she has put a clean nappy on and re-fastened her body suit and she says "Shall we wipe the table together?" Liv rolls over and stands herself up. This takes some time and Tui waits with her hands open, palms facing upwards. Liv puts her hands out for Tui to lift her from the change table. Tui sprays the table and pulls two paper towels. She says "one for me and one for you" and they wipe the table together talking about making it "nice and clean for the next body" and "nice and dry for the next body." They each put their paper towels into the rubbish bin (Tui has to bend down with Liv in her arms so she can reach the bin herself to dispose of her paper towel) *(Observation data transcribed from video)*.

At no point was this interaction rushed and
the example was typical of interactions
between teachers and infants at the case
study centre.

On several occasions I witnessed
teachers allowing children's needs and
rhythms to dictate their break times.
Though the clock suggested a break
time, the teacher would only leave once
the children were settled. The teacher needed
to be satisfied it was an appropriate and convenient
time for the children before they would take a break.

I had noticed the teachers move slowly in the environment
making things seem less hurried and more peaceful in
general so I asked Tui in her interview about this observation
and the following was her answer.

> *The teachers do move slowly and fluidly. We try not to make
> any sudden movements so as not to startle the children. Fluid
> movements create the respectful and peaceful environment and
> we model that to the toddlers so they learn appropriate ways of
> moving and being around the babies (Tui: teacher interview).*

The comment above indicates the teachers' actions are
deliberate and purposeful. Their slow and fluid movements
imply their recognition of the space as one belonging to the
infants and therefore demanding their respect as bigger and
potentially more disruptive beings within that environment.

Wait for a turn

Because there are generally more infants than teachers in
the environment it is essential that infants learn to wait
for a turn. I observed that through teachers' explanations
children were able to wait their turn in the knowledge that
their needs would be attended to as soon as the caregiver
was able. Following is an example of one such interaction.

> Kea is feeding one child. Another child shuffles over and tries to physically get between Kea and the child she is feeding by pulling up on Kea and sliding her hand down Kea's front. Kea explains "I am just helping Duncan with his water – then I will get you some milk." The child sits back down and picks up a nearby silver ball *(Observation transcribed from video).*

It seemed the child was satisfied by Kea's explanation that she would be next and was comfortable to wait for her turn. Teachers also help each other while children are waiting for their intimate caregiving times by soothing the child who is waiting.

> "I know. I know you are getting tired. I can tell. It will be your turn next. OK?" Tui is saying this to Max while she is giving Charlotte her bottle. Kea begins to sing which calms Max while he waits for Tui to give Charlotte her bottle and put her to bed *(Observation data from pen and paper).*

chapter summary

Primary caregiving is not exclusive, not a replacement for parents and, some might say, 'paradoxically' involves a team approach. All members of the team have to be committed to developing and maintaining the primary caregiving system and it involves a deep level of communication, understanding and teamwork between teachers in the environment.

Infants' attachment needs are understood and supported by the close proximity of caregivers in the environment. Infants periodically re-visit their caregiver for emotional reassurance and comfort between periods of independent exploration. This re-visiting of the initial primary caregiver was apparent in the case study centre after children had moved on to an older group and a new primary caregiver. Even after children had gone to school they would re-visit their initial caregiver on return to the centre with a younger sibling.

It is essential that teachers interpret and act on the cues and gestures of infants as this non-verbal communication is the infant's main form of communication. Observing, understanding and responding to these cues and gestures demonstrates to infants that they are valued, important, and capable of making decisions involving their care and education. The use of language for teachers interpreting these cues and gestures is an important aspect of primary caregiving. Teachers use language to explain their actions to infants, to invite interaction with infants and to label emotions or explain how they might interpret an infant's feelings.

Perhaps because of this constant use of language as explanation, infants were able to wait for their turn when the circumstances were communicated to the child. Teachers would take time to communicate carefully with each infant and their use of unhurried time created slow and peaceful interactions between infants and teachers engaged in caregiving routines such as feeding, nappy changing and preparing for rest times. Break times were

not rigidly observed by the clock but rather by the rhythms and needs of the children. Teachers in the environment moved slowly and fluidly so as to reduce their impact on what they considered an environment specifically set up for the needs, pace and nature of infants' development.

Practical guidelines for implementation

Primary caregiving can be successful in your early childhood setting when:

- It is clearly understood and supported by all teachers and parents.

- There is a whole-team approach to its implementation and practice. For example, team members work together to ensure good quality, uninterrupted one-to-one care times are created and maintained.

- Teachers are committed to peaceful observation. This can be difficult if teachers have been conditioned to think that activity is virtuous and peaceful observation may be misconstrued as laziness. Only through peaceful observation will teachers gain in-depth knowledge of each child's intricate cues and gestures.

- Teachers invite children to engage using language and gesture and wait for a gesture of assent from the child prior to engaging in any interaction.

- Teachers are comfortable to be nearby but not intervening unnecessarily, thus allowing each child to solve her own problems as she is able.

- Teachers are comfortable slowing down and not strictly following the clock for routines and break times.

chapter 4

Freedom of movement

Towards a definition

Free movement means allowing children time and space to move and develop at a natural pace and can be summed up with Magda Gerber's caveat, "Never put a baby into a position she cannot get into or out of all by herself." (cited in Hammond, 2009, p. 81). Emmi Pikler initiated the practice of free movement. Pikler's seminal research conducted over many years at Loczy residential nursery showed that typically developing infants (in the orphanage) did not need to be taught how to crawl, sit, stand, or walk (Pikler, 1971). Pikler, and those who have adopted her philosophy, believe that infants must experience all movement for themselves, in their own space and in their own time. Propping an infant to sit, for example, is not allowing him free movement, nor is restricting the child's movement by placing him in a highchair, jolly jumper, walker trainer or similar movement restricting device. The adults' role in all this is simply to observe and not to interfere (Hammond, 2009; Sensory Awareness Foundation, 1994; Gerber, 1998, 2002).

What does the literature say?

While learning during motor development to turn on the belly, to roll, creep, sit, stand and walk, he is not only learning those movements, but also how to learn. He learns to do something on his own, to be interested, to try out, and to experiment. He learns to overcome difficulties. He comes to know the joy and satisfaction which is derived from his success, the result of his patience and persistence (Pikler, 1969, p. 8).

Pikler's research (1963, 1969, cited in Sensory Awareness Foundation, 1994; Association Pikler-Loczy, 2005) involved the systematic observation of infants and young children in attendance at Loczy residential nursery in Budapest. Specifically, nurses responsible for their care and education recorded each child's development and activity with the goal of completing a scientific study of the natural development of infants and small children. Pikler found that children who can move naturally through the developmental milestones (from supine to prone; crawling to sitting; standing to walking to climbing) were not only more able physically but also more able intellectually, socially and emotionally. What Pikler found through systematic observation was that freedom of movement promotes the focus and motivation needed for self-education and gives the infant a lasting view of herself as a competent learner (Association Pikler-Loczy, 2005; Sensory Awareness Foundation, 1994; David & Appell, 2001). These findings were supported by Gerber who argued that freedom of movement can affect infants' dispositions and character (Gerber, 1979). Gerber opines that children may develop a high tolerance or need for stimulation if they are constantly stimulated and entertained. She thinks entertainment may be fun but that the more infants get, the more they want. Once they are used to being entertained by somebody, she thinks, they lose the ability to entertain themselves.

Another devotee of Pikler's motor development research, Janet Gonzalez-Mena, discusses the links between developing motor skills and later learning.

> Through their fascination with their bodies and strong motivation to develop movement, they prove to be highly competent, independent learners. Their persistence to increase movement skills sets a theme for later learning (Janet Gonzalez-Mena, 2009, p. 139).

The adult's role in all of this is to be closely attuned to each child and to facilitate an environment that is stimulating and exciting, but also peaceful and respectful. The adult is there primarily to observe attentively and not to interfere. Gerber (2002) defines this as *wants nothing* time, when the adult wants nothing of the child. The adult is there just to observe with sensitivity. This sensitivity means the adult should also be responsive when a child initiates an interaction during *wants nothing* time.

Money (2006), in her book about infants' natural motor development, inspired by the RIE philosophy, makes the link between moving freely and the child's social and emotional gains.

An infant who is free to move his body toward an object he wants is self-rewarded by a feeling of mastery and develops a can-do attitude toward life that spills over into social, emotional and cognitive realms (Money, 2006, p. 6).

Others investigating free movement have observed joy, self-rewards and social and emotional gains for infants of being allowed to move freely and progress through the typical physical motor development stages without adult intervention (Brownlee, 2009; Gonzalez-Mena, 2009; Cairns-Cowan & McBride, 2009). However, like Money, these are opinion pieces inspired by RIE and Pikler but not based on empirical evidence.

Freedom of movement, or not putting a child into any position he cannot get into or out of by himself, is based on two main ideas: Firstly, the premise that infants should always be laid on their back and not propped to sit or pulled to stand so they can learn to roll, crawl, sit, and stand unaided; and secondly the idea that it can be harmful for infants to be placed in movement restricting devices such as high chairs, walker trainers and jolly jumpers. While there is limited empirical evidence to support the first part of the principle, there is overwhelming support in the available literature for the latter principle regarding movement-restricting devices.

Hannaford (2005), a scientist, educator and the author of a book based on brain development research, writes: "The body plays an integral part in all our intellectual processes" (p. 15).

Movement, a natural process of life, is now understood to be essential to learning; creative thought, high level formal reasoning, and our ability to understand and act altruistically towards all those that share our world (Hannaford, 2005, p. 235).

This evidence would suggest that children who are not restrained in their movements will have greater opportunities for the important intellectual processes outlined above.

As stated previously, infants' learning and development is hampered when they are in car seats or restrictive devices such as baby carriers, belted swings, jolly jumpers, walker trainers and the many other 'containers' available for adult convenience (Gerber, 2002; David & Appell, 2001; Hannaford, 2005; Porter, 2003). The term 'container', to describe the mobility restriction placed upon infants by devices such as these, was coined by Porter who carried out research on movement-restricting devices between 1991 and 1996.

These devices can actually HARM an infant's natural muscular-skeletal development and should NEVER be utilised. In point of fact, they should NEVER have been invented in the first place (Porter, 2003, p.4).

Hannaford (2005) supports this view and is adamant that excessive use of any movement-restricting devices is unwise: "[Such devices] can inhibit active muscular movements either of the neck or core muscles" (p. 111).

Because the majority of research available to support the idea of children progressing naturally through the physical motor development stages without adult intervention originated from a residential nursery, there is an important discussion to be had around the environmental differences between an orphanage setting and family homes and child-

Lachlan
Declan
Levi
Caitlin
Elliott
Welcome
to our space
Genevieve
Annelise

care centres. While the teachers in the case study centre have embraced the free movement philosophy originating from Hungary, they had to adapt the practice of free movement in the centre to fit within a context where children are loved and cared for in family homes while not in attendance at the centre. At the Pikler Institute in Budapest where the children are consistently exposed to the principles of free movement, and the nurses are specifically trained in the approach, one might expect to see entirely different behaviour, consequences and benefits to an early childhood centre where the care is shared between centre and home where the cultural norm may be to 'entertain' the baby. A systematic search of the literature failed to provide any research not completed in orphanages regarding natural motor progression. Further research would be hugely beneficial for early childhood education.

Teacher and parent definitions and views

All teachers involved in my research reported a high level of support for free movement in their interviews.

> *I think freedom of movement means allowing infants and toddlers time and space to explore their body without intimidation or expectations placed upon them. Freedom of movement means exactly that, FREEDOM [interviewee's emphasis] to move and play out all the natural and innate biological need within us all (Tui: teacher interview).*

> *It is essential that we allow children the time and space to learn to move in their own time and at their own pace (Huia: teacher interview).*

> When mums start at our centre and I tell them about free movement they sometimes feel bad that they haven't been doing this at home. So I reassure them that neither did I do this with my children and it is not wrong but that now we know what is best for the child – best for their backs, balance, they fall over less... we must do what we know is best practice for the children. I am definitely going to do it with my grand-children. It does make sense for the respect of the children (Kea: teacher interview).

In each interview I asked teachers what they considered to be the environmental factors essential for promoting free movement for infants. The following were their opinions of the necessary environmental factors.

> The physical and aesthetic environment is very important for the promotion of free movement. Having equipment that is challenging and developmentally appropriate is vital for children's movement and confidence to grow. A clear, uncluttered floor space is needed for infants [who are] learning to be continuously aware of their surroundings to roll and crawl. Steps, ramps, handrails, and the dynamics of the environment encourage and support infants and toddlers to explore and discover the world around them from different perspectives or 'developmental stages'. The environment allows children to understand how and what their bodies can do, or can't. Equipment and resources within the environment should also be well thought out. We minimise mobiles that hang above babies, restricting their motivation to move (Tui: teacher interview).

> Children need space to move – not too many things out at once. No highchairs, jolly jumpers etc. A safe, child-friendly space and comfortable yet challenging, interesting, open ended resources to explore. Peaceful, non-hurried time to practice and support their own development. Encouragement from teachers in the environment (Huia: teacher interview).

> *Space is important and less toys on the floor means more space. It should be a peaceful place. Enough room for lying babies to not be disturbed by walkers and crawlers. Teachers move quietly and slowly to relax the space even further. There are no containers of any kind like jolly jumpers, swings, bouncers, highchairs, tripillows for propping children to sit etc. Also, we have only a few mobiles so there isn't over-stimulation visually in the environment on the ceiling and the walls (Kea: teacher interview).*

To summarise, teachers believed the environmental factors necessary for the promotion of free movement were: The absence of any movement restricting devices such as highchairs, swings and jolly jumpers; clear and uncluttered floor space; a peaceful, non-hurried and supportive environment; challenging and open ended equipment, furnishings and resources to explore; and the deliberate restriction of visually over-stimulating aesthetics and resources such as mobiles.

In the focus group interview, parents were asked about their understanding of the term *freedom of movement*:

- *I think it's about just letting the children learn for themselves and letting them make mistakes and learn from them (Jenny: parent focus group interview).*

- *And everything in their own time (Janine: parent focus group interview).*

- *Not forcing them to do anything they're not ready for developmentally (Vicky: parent focus group interview).*

- *Not restraining or restricting them because it's convenient for you (Janine: parent focus group interview).*

They clearly had a good understanding of the term but differed in their approach to applying this consistently at home:

- *Like this morning when I left and my partner was ironing and watching football. I had to leave and thought … mmm… baby, iron, football, man multi-tasking…. High chair! (Vicky: parent focus group interview)*

- *I followed them [the principles of free movement] to the letter with my first child – and then just practically having babies fifteen months apart I had to bend the rules with Liv.*

Each baby is different and Liv particularly just screamed 24/7 if I lay her on her back. So in the end I had to prop her up because she wasn't happy lying. She was very happy sitting up so I just got over it (Janine: parent focus group interview).

- *We still do the high chair even though he doesn't use it here [at the centre]. I find that he will eat in the high chair a bit more than when we do the dining outside or at the table (Alisa: parent focus group interview).*

Parents generally seem less likely to adopt a strict approach to the philosophy and practices of free movement and this, in turn, has, or is likely to have, an effect on each child's desires to be on their back as opposed to propped to sit. For example a child propped to sit at home may find it difficult to be lying on his or her back at the centre. A child constantly cuddled and held will find it difficult to entertain herself on the floor (Hammond, 2009; Gerber, 1998, 2002).

Teachers support and intervene only when necessary

On several occasions I observed teachers moving toys a little closer to alleviate an infant's frustration. Teachers seemed to interpret the child's body language or cries to mean they were bored or frustrated. Rather than picking the child up they were attempting to enable the child to solve his or her own frustrations through movement and action.

Teachers consciously encouraged independent exploration for infants and were available should the infant indicate they needed physical affection or closeness. It is important to differentiate that this physical affection and closeness was not initiated by the teacher and they would not cuddle a child who they thought was comfortable to otherwise be exploring independently.

Teachers 'over-ride' the rules respectfully

According to the focus group interview and observation data, free movement practices differed between individual families. There were families who had only recently heard of the philosophy and were taking on board some of its values and ideas. Other families felt unable, for whatever reason, to continue with the practices at home. Some families were strictly following the guideline of never putting their child into any position they cannot get into or out of on their own. For each teacher, respect for the individual child and their differing home circumstances defined the terms of practising free movement at the case study centre as highlighted in the following observation.

> Ben is sitting up and Tui says "He doesn't actually sit up by himself but he gets sat up at home and he will often become frustrated with lying down so we sit him up" *(Observation transcribed from pen and paper).*

Since I had observed previously that Ben sometimes became frustrated or disengaged when he was on his back I was not surprised by these comments and actions of the teachers. The teachers (Tui and Kea) are careful to tell me that they think this is more respectful of Ben's wants. It is of interest to note that while the action of propping a child to sit is not in accordance with the philosophy of free movement, if infants have been sat up at home they may become frustrated lying down. *Therefore respect for the child was important above all else.*

From this incident I wondered if Ben prefers sitting up to lying down on his back, how can the teachers be sure that other children would not also have such a preference? When I asked the teachers this they pointed out that he only prefers this as it has been his experience at home. I also wondered if an infant is propped to sit, would he prefer this position? If he is never propped to sit, how could we be sure of his preference? Furthermore, if there is a pattern of children preferring to be sat up once they have experienced this, and there is (Hannaford, 2009; Gerber, 2002), then how do we know we are acting in the child's best interests by always placing them on their backs? Pikler and Gerber would suggest we are acting in the infant's best interests by always laying him on his back to ensure he experiences typical sequential physical motor development (rolling, then crawling, then sitting, then standing). According to Hannaford (2005), children who are propped to sit might possibly skip the important stage of crawling and therefore miss the cross-lateral movement that is so important in overall brain development (Hannaford, 2005). Gerber (1989) says sitting a baby up before he can get in or out of the position on his own teaches a baby to be helpless. Further research would be useful for confirming or negating such statements.

No matter how devoted a teacher is to the principles and practices of free movement, there is no escaping the fact that infants may become frustrated while experiencing free movement. It is the adult who has to decide how strictly they will follow the principles and practices of free movement and whether they might need to 'bend the rules' out of respect for the wishes of the infant.

> Teachers discuss the physical development of the infants and discuss how sometimes Max seems to be frustrated on his tummy. "He can roll onto his tummy but seems to need help sometimes to roll back onto his back where he is sometimes more comfortable" *(Observation data from pen and paper).*

One teacher commented in her interview that often parents are not practicing free movement at home but she felt strongly that they should.

> *I believe that we need to educate more new parents about encouraging their children to spend more time 'on the floor' on their backs exploring their hands, feet, arms and legs (they don't need any other things to begin with like toys, mobiles, exercise gyms to stimulate them). Getting down there with their babies if they are a bit unhappy and talking to them will encourage more 'free movement' instead of propping them up or using other restrictive devices to 'keep them happy' (Huia: teacher interview).*

This opinion is aligned with that of Magda Gerber (1998) who does not believe children get 'bored' when they are in an appropriate environment. Rather, she thinks this is our own projection. Gerber suggests if adults constantly stimulate and entertain infants that they may develop a high tolerance or need for external stimulation. She thinks they should instead be exploring, from the beginning, their own hands and feet.

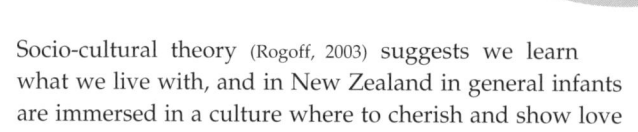

Socio-cultural theory (Rogoff, 2003) suggests we learn what we live with, and in New Zealand in general infants are immersed in a culture where to cherish and show love for an infant we acculturate them with cuddles, love and attention. While elements of the RIE philosophy and Pikler approach believe love and attention are important they are reserved for routine care times and one-to-one interactions which means they are balanced with the need for children to be exploring independently and learning to entertain themselves. Cuddles, love and attention translates into our general culture as what Gerber might have referred to as interfering or smothering.

Analysis of data from my research was unable to confirm or negate the free movement principles and practices. This was a surprising finding and certainly lays a challenge for further research into free movement within an early childhood setting or family home. Instead of confirming the need for infants to progress unaided through the natural motor development stages, my research questioned and explored the idea of adaptation versus adoption of a philosophy. The teachers at the case study centre had clearly adapted the principles of free movement as they would 'over-ride' these principles if they felt it was the most respectful action for the child.

My mentor and teacher, Norah Fryer, a practitioner with some forty years of experience, including time learning and studying with Magda Gerber, recently said:

> *Over the past forty years, having been involved in the study and practice of early childhood education and care I have observed many 'methods' whose passionate followers truly believe it is 'the way.' What I now understand is that it is not the 'method' but the daily respectful interactions that teachers demonstrate through their knowledge, skill and attitude that becomes both the foundation and the framework for their pedagogical values... [Teachers display] intentional nurturing and teaching and it is the 'person' within the teacher and the 'respect' within the method which can enhance or diminish the quality* (N. Fryer, personal communication, July, 2010).

Norah's words highlighted for me the idea of 'respect' being an over-all driver of the philosophy at the case study centre. The teachers are passionate advocates of the RIE philosophy and Pikler approach, but in translating these methods to their centre environment they have adapted the principles and practices out of respect for the families and infants for whom they care.

Peaceful observation

Wants nothing time was identified in the literature (Gerber, 1984) as time when the teacher wants nothing of the child. This means the teacher is not engaging in a routine care time, neither is he or she initiating any kind of activity with the child. The following were examples of *wants nothing time* from the observations made in my study:

> Kea carries Max in and lays him gently on his back in the nursery. She gives him a soft toy which he discards and he is content to babble and play with his own hands and feet while she puts away his bottles. When Kea returns she sits near Max but doesn't speak or interfere. She is just watching Max *(Observation data from pen and paper)*.

Liv and Max are in the nursery and Charlotte is asleep. Tui sits between the two children who are awake and Kea goes to have a break. Max is happy on his tummy kicking his feet and waving his arms and babbling – he is moving himself ever so slightly backwards. Liv is drawing on a piece of paper and eating a piece of bread at the same time. This play is uninterrupted for some time (more than five minutes) and the environment is very quiet. Tui is simply observing the children (Observation data from pen and paper).

More recently, Da Ros and Wong (1996) have described this approach as "providing a secure base" (p. 216). They consider that being fully present with young children provides an opportunity to actively observe the children and reflect on their progress, language, and interests without needing to intervene in the infant's current explorations. Gonzalez-Mena and Widmeyer Eyer (2007) suggest that being fully available and responsive but not intervening is a skill most adults need to learn. From my observation I am going to label this phenomena *peaceful observation*. It is *peaceful* as it is quiet and no-one is making any demands of another person. This is a time when the teacher simply observes the child in order to reach a greater level of individual understanding.

It can be a challenge for teachers who are used to being busy all the time to simply sit and observe children peacefully.

> *In our society, we're trained to do, do, do. And if you don't, you pretend to do, do, do. You must act as if you are very busy, because being busy is virtuous. Not doing anything is considered laziness.... Nobody talks about being observant. The more we do, the busier we are, the less we really pay attention (Gerber, 2002, p. 63).*

The practice of paying attention demonstrates an additional way of showing that we really care. We can stop long enough to clear our mind of what we *think* they might need or want and see what the child is communicating about what he or she *actually* needs or wants. This peaceful observation time may be something that takes some getting used to, particularly if teachers have been working in large, busy settings where the perception is that activity equals good work and, as Gerber challenged, inactivity equals laziness.

> *We often make snap judgements about what a child is thinking or feeling, and they may be completely inaccurate. If we sit back and continue to observe, we get the opportunity to watch as events unfold, and children are able to follow through with their own ideas* (Leon-Weil and Hewitt, 2008, p. 26).

As adults, perhaps we have become culturally conditioned as Gerber (2002) suggests, believing that being busy means we are being productive and virtuous. If we are not constantly talking at infants does it mean we are perceived as indifferent?

We are not indifferent when we just notice, it is just that we are respectful enough not to offer support until the child needs it" (Brownlee, 2009, p. 4).

When teachers observe peacefully they are being productive, they are not indifferent, on the contrary, they are highly attuned to the individual capabilities, needs and desires of the child they are observing.

Adoption versus adaptation of a philosophy

When a philosophy is *adopted* it is embraced, believed and practised in its purest original form. This can have unintended or unexpected consequences when the philosophy is transferred to an entirely new context. We know that socio-cultural context is inextricably linked to learning and development (Rogoff, 2003). Therefore, we should not expect that the same philosophy practised in two different contexts would yield the same outcome.

This leads us to *adaptation* of a philosophy which is when the essence of a philosophy is believed and followers adapt the practices to suit the individual cultural context into which it is being transferred.

> It is important that early childhood educators consider and reflect on current trends rather than hurriedly and carelessly adopt a trend, although a concept or trend should not be denied merely because it seems new. It is important to assess each idea, programme and innovation to determine its worth and applicability to the children's culture and community (Saracho and Spodek, 2003, p. 182).

Gerber *adopted* Pikler's approach and took it from an orphanage in Hungary to parents in Los Angeles. She suggests: "I have felt sometimes like the bridge between Dr. Pikler and American society" (Gerber, 1998, p. 189). Teachers at the case study centre have *adapted* the Pikler approach and RIE philosophy to ensure they are a good fit with the cultural context of the centre and families who attend.

A surprising finding was the way teachers did not practise the principles of free movement strictly. Parents did not either, even when they knew the principles. I believe this is a result of transferring a philosophy from an orphanage, where nurses are trained in the principles and children are present twenty-four hours a day, seven days a week, to a childcare centre setting, where teachers believe strongly in the principles but children are essentially in a shared care situation and are returning to family homes each evening and weekend. Children who have parents in this culture, by the very nature of being part of a family, will generally be picked up and cuddled, they might be propped up, pulled up, and bounced around and this does not fit with the principles and practices of free movement.

Parents considered there were limitations of practising free movement at home. Most parents present at the focus group interview reported their use of high chairs at home. This practice of restraining a child for the purpose of adult convenience was discussed as something that is "practical in a busy household." Some found managing mealtimes without a high chair too difficult or had already started using one before they were exposed to the centre's philosophy. We also learned that some of the children were propped to sit at home. Not many parents described their reasons, but for at least one the rationale was that the child became unsettled lying on her back. The parent, who had an older child she had raised strictly following the principles of free movement, was not practising these as strictly with her second child. Her rationale for propping her younger daughter to sit was that she felt her child was becoming anxious (perhaps not feeling safe?) on her back as there was a fifteen month old toddler (the older sibling) present in the environment.

Further enquiry into the relevance and possible benefits of practising free movement in early childhood settings in New Zealand would be beneficial. It is important to evaluate and monitor innovations when they have been transplanted into another context as these may not fit well within local context and may not have the same outcomes as at the original site (Slaveron, Arney & Scott, 2006; Saracho & Spodek, 2003).

Chapter summary

Freedom of movement is a term understood as meaning never putting a child into a position she cannot get into or out of all by herself. There are two aspects to this premise: one is not interfering in any way with the natural motor progression of the infant (for example, from lying on his back, to rolling, then crawling, then sitting, and eventually pulling himself up and standing); the other premise is not putting children in any type of container, such as a high chair, walker-trainer, belted swing or jolly-jumper. In the literature freedom of movement is associated with benefits to children's physical, emotional, and cognitive functioning. However, a lack of empirical evidence to support natural motor progression when applied to children developing normally in family homes was identified in this chapter. This led me to examine the literature on adaptation versus adoption of a philosophy which, along with further research recommendations, was also discussed in this chapter.

… # chapter 5

Respect

Towards a definition

Respect is "a fundamental human value that forms the basis of character and personality" (Miller & Pedro, 2006, p. 293). Respect is deeply embedded in the philosophy and practices at the case study centre. Teachers engage in ways that would suggest they accept each person as an individual with rights and freedoms. They are prepared to receive each person without them being who the teacher might want them to be. This is evident when teachers interact with children, when they interact with each other, and when they interact with families who come into the environment.

What does the literature say?

One element of respect according to Te One (2008) is to consider the rights of children. "Children's rights do not receive widespread public or political support in New Zealand" (Smith, 2007, p. 1). Article 12 of the United Nations Convention on the Rights of the Child states: "The child has the right to express his or her opinion freely and to have that opinion taken into account in any matter or procedure affecting the child" (United Nations Committee on the Rights of the Child, 2003). However, adults do not always see infants as capable of having an opinion and often matters or procedures affecting the child are simply decided by adults responsible for the child (Te One, 2008).

According to Brownlee (2008), some of the general practices taken for granted with infants and toddlers are actually very disrespectful when we examine them more deeply. Picking children up without telling them, washing a face in a hurry, dressing a child without talking through what you are doing are just a few examples of minimal respect. Brownlee argues that just because an infant or toddler has less ability to verbally communicate their desires does not mean they are any less confident or competent than any other human being (Brownlee, 2008).

Gonzalez-Mena (2009) is in agreement with Brownlee and considers one aspect of respect to be predictability, which is helping babies anticipate what will happen next. Babies should know what to expect each step of the way when they are being dressed, changed, washed, groomed or fed (Gerber, 1984). Predictability leads to a sense of security for babies.

If we think about it as adults we know what we are doing, why we are doing it, where we are going and what we are doing next (generally). Surely spelling this out for children is a simple matter of respect.

Respect is shown when adults treat children in ways similar to how they would like to be treated by others.

This is the golden rule of quality care. If a person comes up behind adults unexpectedly and touches them, the first reaction is one of surprise. People may jump or flinch. Adults expect to be informed when someone is about to touch them. Therefore, teachers and other adults show respect when they approach an infant or toddler by moving in front, so the child sees someone is coming. Then respectful adults speak and tell the child what is going to happen (Cheshire, 2007, p. 36).

Because human beings tend to treat others as they have been treated (Bowlby, 1988), teachers need to model empathy. If we were always instructed about what will happen for, with and to us, rather than consulted with and respected as an individual with rights and freedoms, then we would feel powerless and insignificant. When a child is treated with empathy he or she will learn empathy towards others.

Reporting on her doctoral thesis, Te One (2010) states that if we knew more about children's rights, we would be better advocates for the principles of high quality early childhood practices.

The biggest barriers to understanding children's rights are adult misconceptions that children lack the capacity to make sensible decisions; that children's rights undermine adult authority; and, that complying with children's rights requires too much effort (Te One, 2010, p. 8).

These misconceptions can lead adults to neglect the relationship factor in education. James L Hymes Jr, wrote prolifically from the 1930's to the 1980's on the need for adults to understand and regard children's socio-emotional needs. His belief was that the foundation for true education is relationship based.

> *What matters most when you're three, four, six or eight – I'm afraid it's what matters most while 12, 79 and so on – it's PEOPLE* (Hymes, 1975, cited in Anderson, 2009, p. 14).

This idea of relationship-based learning is at the heart of respect for children's confidence and competence as well as primary caregiving with infants.

If we are to truly understand the relationship-based potential for education of infants then we need to develop greater empathy and slow down. Being fully attentive and slow enough to pick up on the individual rhythms and cues of the child is a highly skilled task. In her article: "Time", Raewyne Bary (2009) asserts: "Relationship building takes time. It can't be hurried and it cannot be programmed into a daily roster system" (p. 19). She suggests: "Maybe we should follow their sense of time…. To be in the moment: to be in the space of time and let go of the ticking clock. Let the infants and toddlers lead us. Let's follow their rhythm, instead of that of the ticking clock" (p. 18). Bary also recommends four key elements for the development of trusting relationships between children, teachers and families:

- *Being available*
- *Being tuned in*
- *Being responsive*
- *Being consistent*

All of the above requirements have one thing in common, and that is the need for time (Bary, 2009, p. 18).

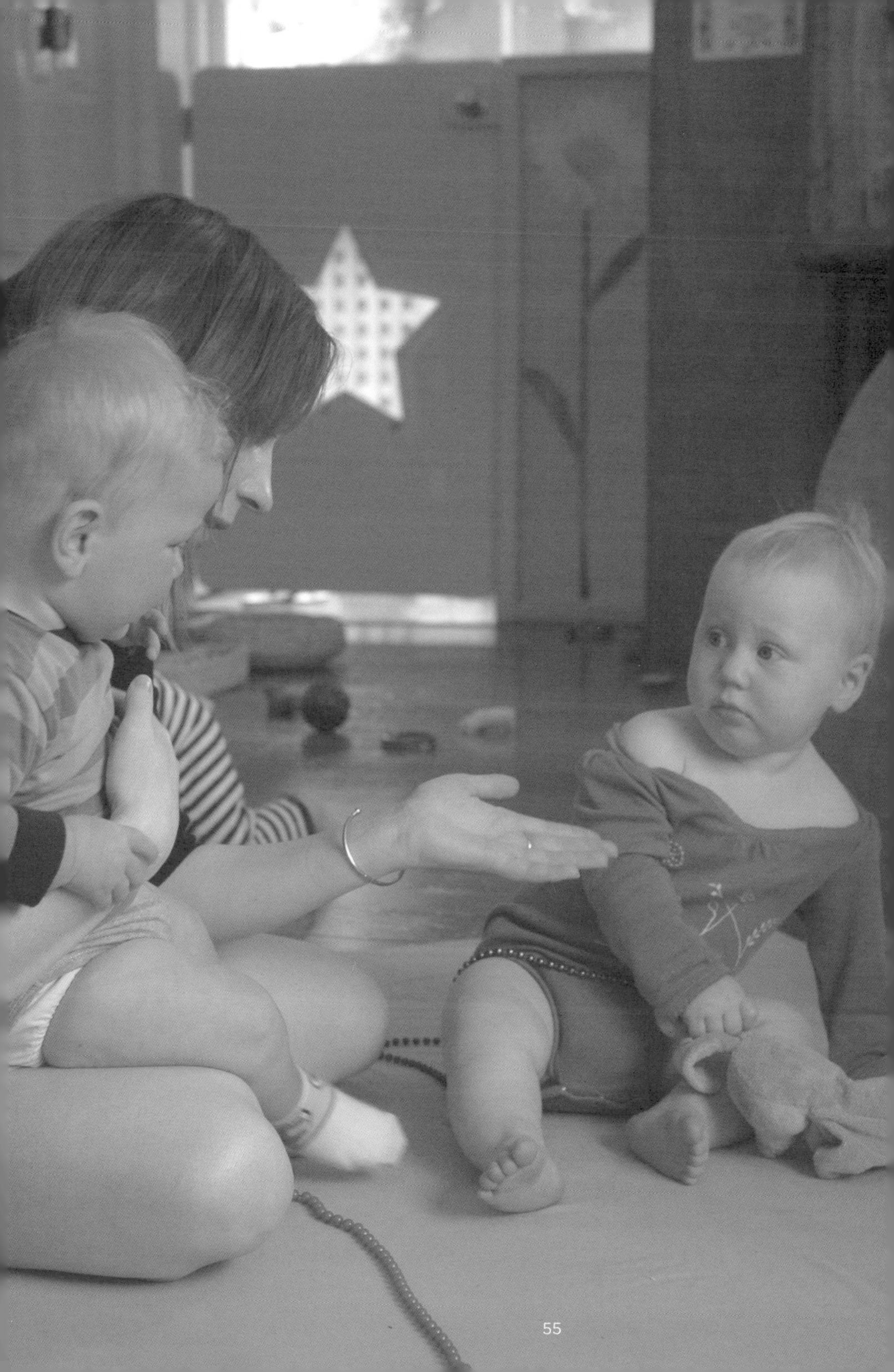

Unhurried time may prove central to showing respect for infants. Responding with sensitivity and developing nurturing relationships both involve the use of unhurried time. These two aspects are the first two of eleven ways Stacie Goffin (1990) argues we can show our respect when interacting with children. Showing respect for childhood, she believes, involves the following:

1. *Responding with sensitivity to children's individuality*
2. *Developing nurturing relationships with children*
3. *Using adult authority with wisdom to facilitate children's growth into caring adults*
4. *Considering how day-to-day practices influence children*
5. *Recognising discipline as a learning experience for children and viewing mistakes as potential learning opportunities*
6. *Acknowledging children's competencies*
7. *Organising a curriculum that provides children with interesting things to think about*
8. *Supporting and strengthening parents in their childrearing responsibilities*
9. *Acknowledging the expertise needed to be a professional in early childhood education*
10. *Speaking out on behalf of early childhood education as a profession*
11. *Speaking out on behalf of children's needs to parents, school administrators, business and community representatives, and policy makers (pp. 37-40).*

I agree with each of Goffin's guidelines and consider two points particularly noteworthy in relation to respect for children's confidence and competence. "Acknowledging children's competencies" suggests that we must consider the child as capable. We must view him as able and resist the urge to do too much for the child and, instead, allow ourselves the time to see what he can accomplish on his own. Gerber's assertion: "Do less; observe more; enjoy most" (quote displayed on the wall at the case study centre) is in agreement with Goffin. The second of Goffin's respectful 'ways' that really resonated with me in relation to my research was: "Responding with sensitivity to children's individuality." This means considering a person's decisions, choices, preferences and styles of responding and interacting to be valid even when they are different to your own.

Ethics of care

The notions of empathy and respect are at the heart of the 'ethics of care' discourse prevalent in the feminist moral theory literature (Goldstein, 1998; Dahlberg & Moss, 2005; Noddings, 1984; Tronto, 1993). The general premise of the ethics of care debate is that "caring is not something you are, but rather something you engage in, something you do" (Goldstein, 1998, p. 247). The word 'care', as it pertains to teaching, is often linked to feelings, personality traits, or a person's temperament. However, Goldstein argues, this simplistic view of care obscures the "complexity and intellectual challenge of work with young children" (p. 245).

Noddings (1984) is in agreement with Goldstein and states: "Caring involves stepping out of one's own personal frame of reference and into the other's" (p. 24). Noddings calls this motivational shift of putting aside your own choices, preferences, ideas, and really receiving another person as "motivational displacement" (p. 24). This shift "compels the one-caring to give primacy, even if momentarily, to the goals and needs of the cared-for" (Goldstein, 1998, p. 246). This motivational displacement coupled with peaceful observation will lead the one caring to support the one cared for in a manner most suited to the cared for. For example, a teacher may believe that a child has no need or use for a security toy, but in reading the gestures and cues of the infant (peaceful observation) may offer the infant their security toy against their own beliefs (motivational displacement).

Noddings (1984) proposes that each caring encounter will be unique, situated and variable: "The actions of [the] one-caring will be varied rather than rule-bound, predictable in the global sense but unpredictable in detail" (p. 24). For instance, a teacher who believes that children should progress naturally through the stages of motor development will predictably lay a child gently on his back to explore. Perhaps unpredictably, she might then prop this child to sit (motivational displacement) if he becomes upset lying on his back (peaceful observation). Responsibility, communication, attentiveness, competence, responsiveness, empathy, intuition, compassion, love, and commitment are all attributes described by the various researchers contributing to our understanding of the 'ethics of care'.

Teachers invite children to engage

Interactions with children at the case study centre would most often begin with some form of invitation by the teacher. Usually this would take the form of a verbal invitation accompanied by outstretched open hands with palms facing up. After this initial verbal and physical invitation, the caregiver would wait for a response. The response time from the child varied. The one constant in this sequence of events was that nothing happened until the child agreed.

> Interaction between Kea and Charlotte: "Would you like a nappy change?" she says the words and offers opened arms and hands. When Charlotte doesn't react Kea says "I'll wait until you are ready." "You let me know when you are ready" Charlotte thought for about 30 seconds and then bum-shuffled, waving her hands over to Kea who scooped her into her waiting open hands and arms and took her for a nappy change *(Observation data transcribed from video).*

In this exchange the child is offered the choice and therefore holds the power over when her nappy is changed. This was very typical of the interactions at the centre. A teacher would initiate with a verbal invitation, always accompanied by open hands held out as a gesture of invitation. Then the teacher would wait for the child's assent which would usually be a physical sign such as tipping forwards into the open arms or putting their hands up to be carried or moving closer to be picked up.

When we discussed this at the parent focus group we found there were clear differences between interactions at the centre and at home. It was apparent that the intimate care times at home were more rushed than those at the centre. Being rushed can be unsettling and undermining to the self-esteem of the infant (Kovach & Da Ros-Voseles, 2008). It was also evident that children had less control over the situation, for example whether they had a choice about lying down or standing up to be changed. The following quotes are taken from the wall displays at the case study centre:

> "The care moment is the most important moment in a baby's life" – Dr. Emmi Pikler.

> "When the experience is a pleasant one, they will be willing to participate again... and again... and again!"

> "Freedom to move, responsive reciprocal relationships, making their own choices, working together, partnership and cooperation during care."

An invitation and explanation is a simple matter of respect. Imagine being asked, being heard, and holding the power in matters affecting your physical well-being. For most adults this is accepted as a basic human right. Now imagine someone physically lifting or interfering with you in anyway to which you have not consented. In the second instance, when you were not invited or consulted, the experience is one of powerlessness. You might feel more like an object rather than a human with individual thoughts, opinions, freedoms and rights.

> When an adult speaks quietly about what is happening and waits for a response, the child does not need to be on alert that a change could be coming at any moment unannounced (Hammond, 2009, p. 17).

Unhurried time

In order to give infants unhurried time, teachers have to make a commitment to slow down and be emotionally present with infants (Kovach & Da Ros-Voseles, 2008). The following is an example of how teachers were unhurried in their interactions with infants at the case study centre.

When Tui comes back to the nursery Kea has been cuddling Max and Tui heats his bottle. She gently removes his jersey. This is a slow process and she talks to him about how she is moving his body. Tui takes Max and the bottle through to the sleep room. Tui cuddles Max as she feeds him his bottle. Ben is not yet asleep and he calls out when Max makes some sounds prior to his bottle coming. Max stops to have a look at the moving stars and Tui waits patiently until he wants his bottle again. She tries again but Max moves his head indicating he has had enough. "OK shall we put you to bed then?" She puts Max into his bed and strokes his head. She hums along with the music that is playing and Max makes little snuffling sleepy noises while she hums. He plays with her hand which is not stroking his head. Ben lets out some sounds and Max makes a small complaint, not enough for Tui to take him out of bed. Max yawns and Tui rubs his chest gently. Max experiments with sounds and Ben joins in a little bit. Now Tui is rubbing his chest gently with one hand and his head with the other. Max' eyes close and Tui stays with him a while longer continuing to rub his chest. When she is sure he's asleep she gently removes her hand from his chest and fluidly secures the side of his cot and removes herself from his cot. She sits listening to Ben for a while. I think she is deciding whether she should allow him to see her as till this point though he has heard her he hasn't seen her. He holds his hands out to Tui to indicate that he needs her. She picks him up and suggests they go and change his nappy *(Observation data transcribed from video)*.

The observation above is evidence of the teacher's commitment to slowing down and providing valuable, uninterrupted, quality time and attention with the infant. When she does this she demonstrates her ability to empathise with the infant and understand from his perspective what the experience of going to sleep at the centre must feel like. A supporting piece of documentation demonstrating that this is a conscious decision on the part of the teacher is a wall display in the infant room (see over page).

T	Tender
I	Intimate
M	Moments
E	Every day
T	Try
I	Imagining
M	Meaningful
E	Experiences from a child's perspective

Norah Fryer & Rangi Ruru Early Childhood College students 1993

One parent at the focus group interview described a workshop (run by the teachers at the case study centre) where she and her husband, along with other partners present, had to feed each other:

> We were role playing and one was the child and the other the adult and we had to role play the scenario where they are rushing the child. Her partner was feeding her yoghurt and talking on his cell phone at the same time and wasn't allowing her the time to swallow. She said by the end of it she was covered in yoghurt and really angry but the exercise taught her a great lesson about following the child's lead for when they are ready and how long they might need to swallow etc. Also, she was annoyed about him talking on the cell phone instead of paying attention to her (Janine: parent focus group interview).

Another aspect of unhurried time is the conscious decision that teachers have made to move slowly and fluidly in the infant room. They move as though they do not want to disturb anything. On several occasions I observed teachers moving slowly and softly, with small, quiet, and fluid movements. When asked about this in the teacher interviews they would explain their intention is to reinforce the idea that this is a children's space and teachers do not want to do anything that will disturb that slow, peaceful space and pace.

This practice of taking adequate time deepens teachers' awareness and knowledge of each child, sensing by their behaviour, body language and expressions. In the example earlier in this chapter, the cues suggested Max might be a bit tired. Talking to him about tiredness and suggesting a sleep allowed the child to be the decision maker in the process.

My research indicated that when teachers give their time they show value for the person with whom they are engaged. When we rush an interaction we run the risk of leaving the person with whom we are interacting feeling unsatisfied and undervalued by the experience. Each child will have his or her own rhythm and pace. Respectful practice involves stepping out of our own rhythm and pace and adjusting to that of the infant. For adults generally this is going to mean slowing down a great deal in order to observe and interpret needs, invite children to engage, wait for their response and then engage in the interaction at the child's pace.

Choices are offered

On several occasions I observed teachers offering children choices and one of the most common was to offer children a choice in the colour of the bib they wanted to wear for a mealtime. This was something that happened prior to every meal time and was part of a sequenced routine for children. Wearing a bib indicated that they would have their meal next. I noticed that the action of choosing a bib aided children's ability to wait for a turn. The bib choosing exercise was a cue to the child that once they have a bib it follows that they will be having their meal next.

At mealtimes there were always choices for food prepared by the cook so teachers could cater to children's individual tastes. Also choices about when children were hungry and wanted to eat were decided by the child. Teachers would offer food and if it was not accepted they would put it away to offer later.

Teachers at the case study centre felt that offering children choices was an essential element of their philosophy and practices. Below are examples of the centre manager's opinion on the subject of choices.

> *It is important to offer children choices. You know especially infants — they don't get a lot of choice about anything really. So offering them a choice in anything that involves them gives the power over to them. They can see and feel how powerful they are in decisions which directly affect their wellbeing (Huia: teacher interview).*
>
> *Talking to them about what is going to happen next and giving them the opportunity to respond and be a willing participant. Giving children choices (particularly infants who are often overlooked in this area), they will soon get the idea that their opinion is valued (Huia: teacher interview).*

In agreement, Leon-Weil and Hewitt (2008) found "when we involved children in the decisions that affected their lives, they reached a different level of critical thinking and expression" (p. 25).

A parent who has adopted the philosophy of the centre at home agreed about the importance of offering choices. Janine made the following observation at the parent focus group interview:

It was in offering choices that I realised one shirt was actually uncomfortable to get over my son's head. When I offered the choice he wouldn't choose that one and that was why (Janine: parent focus group interview).

Offering choices and inviting children to engage are both important parts of the programme provided at the case study centre. In both of these aspects the teachers consider it essential that they wait for a response. Suskind (1985, cited in Petrie & Owen, 2005, p. 144) calls this time between teacher invitation and child response *tarry time*. This is another important aspect of offering choices which links to the concept of unhurried time. When a choice is offered, teachers need to allow time for a response (and this may take longer than expected in 'adult time') and then react according to the wishes of the child.

Giving children choices shows them that educators care. When educators trust children to make choices concerning their daily events and activities, they not only create a sense of autonomy, but also an environment of respect (Brumbaugh, 2008, p. 175).

Peaceful observation

My findings indicate that through subtle signs and gestures in the presence of sensitive, attuned observers, even the youngest child can express his or her opinion and therefore have his or her human rights upheld (United Nations Committee on the Rights of the Child, 2003).

It is through observation that teachers learn what the child wants, needs, likes, dislikes and also what they are capable of and what their emerging capabilities are. This peaceful observation enables teachers to go further than feeling empathy. They go beyond "what would I want if I were her?" to actually consider "what does she want?" An example was when Kea put away a child's pacifier because she had thought she did not need it.

> The child didn't complain but looked anxious so Kea gave it back and said "Do you feel you need that?" Liv put it down beside her and continued to explore without it (observation transcribed from video).

In the example above, Kea felt Liv had no need or use for the pacifier but by paying close attention to the emotions of the child who did not complain but simply looked anxious, was able to interpret the desires of the child. The ethics of care discourse (Goldstein, 1998; Noddings, 1984) would suggest that peaceful observation led Kea to give Liv the pacifier against her own better judgment (motivational displacement) because the ethics of care involve respecting another person enough to understand what they might *actually want* as opposed to what you *think they might want*.

This ability to really see from the perspective of another requires close attention on the part of the teacher. On one of the walls in the infant environment there is a large picture of a key and inside the key are the words "Just notice." I found that teachers in the environment were very good at noticing what was happening for each child.

> Full attention is focused and it neither judges nor labels. It just notices. Every little thing... full attention allows you to be in the present moment, exactly as all infants are, all of the time (Brownlee, 2009, p. 4).

Our adult lives are crowded with time schedules and plans. We are always thinking ahead or planning ahead but an infant demonstrates how to be fully present in each moment.

Teachers support rather than intervene

The teachers at the case study centre all felt very strongly that support rather than intervention was a mark of respect for the child. They felt that adults generally try to do too much for children and this can have a damaging affect on the child's perception of herself as a confident and competent learner. The following were some of the comments from the teacher interviews.

> *Our infants are exposed to an environment that respects them for who they are, their wairua is nurtured, honoured and celebrated. Our programme encourages our babies to feel secure and safe to make independent choices in all areas of their learning and development. I believe this teaches them a positive and healthy self-image and, ultimately and optimistically, a healthy world view (Tui: teacher interview).*

I think respecting children's confidence and competence provides them with the mana that comes with working through feelings and emotions. When infants are allowed time and support to work through feelings like frustration they learn to self-regulate, collect themselves and focus. They also learn to trust and feel emotionally secure if they need that extra hand from someone else. Knowing when to lend that hand is really important. Children are capable of so much more than people often give them credit for (Tui: teacher interview).

[We believe in] giving children the freedom, and encouraging them to become confident explorers. Being there to support, but not interfere as they figure things out, for example how to use their own bodies to get to where they want to go in their own time (Huia: teacher interview).

Parents also valued the idea of support rather than intervention for the healthy development of self-esteem. When I asked what is it to respect children's competence the parents at the focus group had the following definitions:

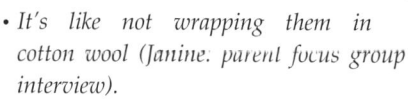

- *It's not stepping in too early to allow them to learn and master things on their own. He's doing what he thinks he can do and I shouldn't be the one to decide what that is. It's respecting that he will figure it out himself — and he might fall off and he might get hurt but it's allowing that as a learning thing (Alisa: parent focus group interview).* 
- *It's like not wrapping them in cotton wool (Janine: parent focus group interview).*

- *Trying to let him work it out for himself. When they work it out themselves they get a huge sense of satisfaction (Jenny: parent focus group interview).*

From these comments it was apparent that parents felt children learn from their mistakes and have a greater sense of mastery and autonomy when they are able to try things on their own. One parent told a story about a playgroup:

- *At this playgroup I watched my son negotiate the steps without any help and get a bike which he then careened off and grazed his head. He was a bit sore so he cried for me to comfort him and I went to give him a cuddle. What I loved was that he calmed so quickly and was determined to get back on the bike and continue mastering it. There was another mother watching who wouldn't allow her child to come out because she'd just seen what had happened. I was sad for her and her child because she was being overly anxious and her child would be denied a great learning experience (Alisa: parent focus group interview).*

- *In the morning we like to make muffins and loaf and things like that and my two children really like to help. I tell them that the knife is really sharp and you can tell they know what that means and I explain that the element is really hot and they learn and understand. Having them bake with me is obviously messier and more time consuming but they are learning so much and gain a sense of confidence and competence about being part of the creation. But it's not dangerous – it's just really messy! (Janine: parent focus group interview).*

- *Yes, I think you can do something for a child so much, but there is nothing like the satisfaction and learning that is cemented when someone does something for themselves or accomplishes something by themselves (Vicky: parent focus group interview).*

These were all important points the parents brought up. They talked about offering their child support. In the case of the child with the bike at the playgroup it was in the form of a cuddle when he fell off. In the case of the children who help with baking the support was in the form of telling them that the knife is sharp and the element is hot. The parents did not intervene, however, stopping them from riding the bike or baking the muffins, and thereby allowed the child the sense of achievement and competence that comes with accomplishing a task autonomously.

Brownlee (2009) talks about "a baby's sacred quest for competence" and discusses why trusting children and waiting and watching is far more beneficial to the child than rushing in to save or rescue them. When a child learns to master anything on their own there is a sense of power and competence that no amount of watching an adult do it for them could possibly hope to emulate.

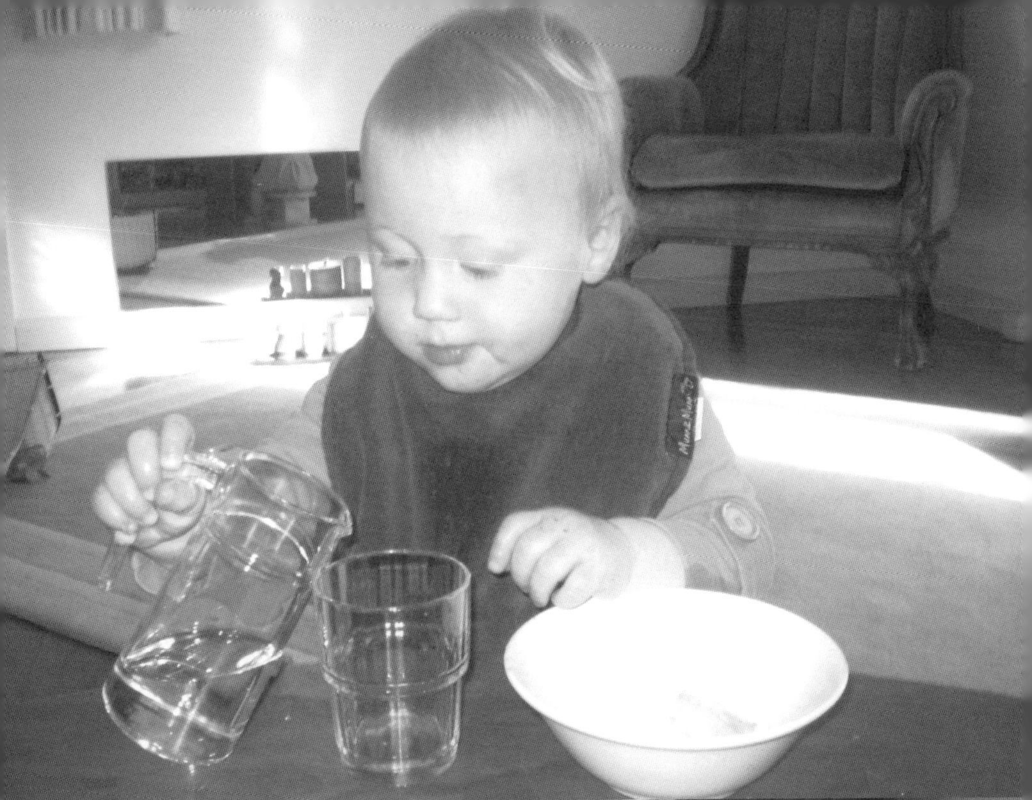

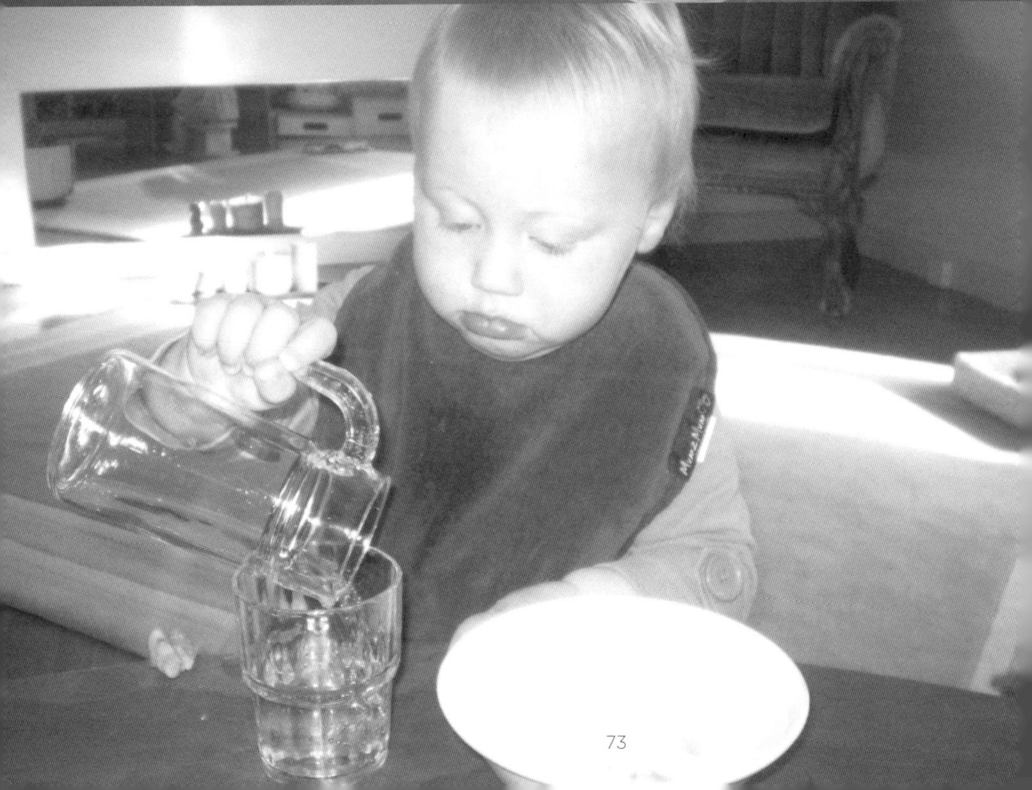

A team approach is an important element

Respect is evident between teachers, as well as between teacher and child and teacher and parent. Teachers display respectful relationships with each other and have developed some sound strategies for ensuring they have a shared understanding of what it is to be respectful of each other. The team contract created by the current teaching team at the case study centre is a good example:

- *We will maintain our support for one another, valuing each other's individuality, friendships and bring out the best in each other.*

- *We will always remember the importance of our parents and whānau community and respect and value their contribution, knowledge and beliefs.*

- *We will take pride in our environment and show our respect for the children's learning by tidying and resetting relevant learning opportunities for the children during the day.*

- *We will aim to keep our display boards up to date, beautiful and meaningful for our children, parents and families.*

- *Before talking with another teacher, we will first consider the situation and relevance, and be respectful of teachers and children involved in special moments.*

- *When returning to the room we will keep dialogue open and remember to ask teachers in the room "where are we at?" or "what can I do?" When leaving an area we will exchange any important information with teachers remaining in the room.*

- *We will all contribute to 'housekeeping-type' jobs, putting equipment and resources back in the correct places, keeping the washing up to date and clearing the kitchen.*

- *We will show our respect for nature and animals by looking after the needs of our smallest residents, Pinny and Gig (the centre guinea-pigs), and allowing the children to be a part of their care.*

- *We will recycle / reuse / reduce and think about ways in which we can be kind to the environment wherever we can (case study centre team contract, December, 2009).*

This team contract is a document the teachers developed together by brainstorming everything that each felt was important. Everything in the contract had to be agreed to by all the parties and this has given the teachers shared understanding of respectful behaviour, a common reference point when boundaries are pushed and most importantly, because it was worked out together, each of the team has ownership of the ideas the contract contains.

The teachers at the case study centre have a vision about how their centre should feel and what experiences will be like for infants and toddlers who come to their centre. The most important part of realising this vision is that every one of the teaching team shares the vision. Part of the philosophy with children is that teachers trust them to be confident and competent learners but the first level of trust necessary within the environment is among the adults as demonstrated by the team contract.

Chapter summary

Actions demonstrating respect include predictability, empathy, developing nurturing relationships, considering the child as a capable and equal human being, being fully present and engaged with each child and observing and responding sensitively. Respect involves intentional caring, or an ethic of care where the teacher is intentionally able to displace his or her own motivation in order to truly understand the needs and wishes of the child and act accordingly.

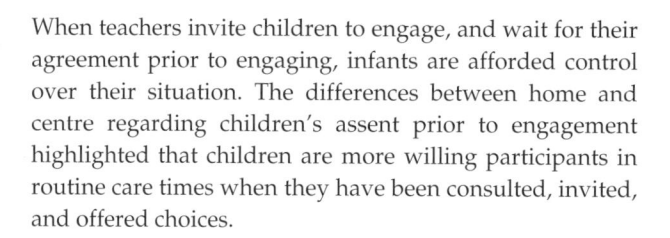

When teachers invite children to engage, and wait for their agreement prior to engaging, infants are afforded control over their situation. The differences between home and centre regarding children's assent prior to engagement highlighted that children are more willing participants in routine care times when they have been consulted, invited, and offered choices.

Teachers at the case study centre have made a commitment to slowing down and being emotionally present with each child. This provides the infant with valuable, uninterrupted, quality time and attention. It also provides the teacher with a deepened awareness and knowledge of each child.

Another aspect of unhurried time includes the way teachers move slowly and fluidly within the environment so as not to disturb the peaceful, age-appropriate space and pace. The final aspect of unhurried time observed was that teachers took their breaks according to the needs and rhythms of the children instead of according to the clock.

Teachers were available to the children at all times but resisted any unnecessary intervention. This, they felt, contributed to each child's view of themselves as a confident and competent learner. Teachers would pay close attention to each child and offered their support when it was requested. They valued each child's sense of autonomy and accomplishment, which led them to offer support without doing something for a child which they thought the child was capable of achieving on their own.

The respectful interactions between teachers and infants were replicated in other relationships throughout the environment. Teachers showed respect for each other through their interactions and teaching practices, and respect was also evident between teachers and parents. Interactions at all levels were respectful, and this culture of respect influenced the actions and reactions of people in the environment.

Practical guidelines for implementation

We can show our respect for infants in early childhood centres by:

- Recognising that infants need to develop a strong and reciprocal relationship with at least one other person in the environment and implementing a primary caregiver system to cater for that primary need.

- Inviting infants to engage and waiting for their approval prior to interacting with them.

- Interpreting children's intentions by peacefully observing them and paying close attention to their body language, cues and gestures.

- Slowing down and recognising that infants may prefer an unhurried approach to their individual care routines, learning and development. This includes being flexible about breaks and making them work according to the needs and rhythms of the infants as opposed to working by the clock.

- Offering infants choices about what is happening for them and waiting for a response to the choices we have offered.

- Being available to the infant and supporting them in their learning, but resisting the urge to intervene unnecessarily in their problem-solving efforts and mastery of their own physical development.

- Recognising the need for a strong philosophy and deep level of respect among team members. We can accomplish more and achieve greater quality for the benefit of the infants in our care when we share the same goals as a team, communicate effectively and demonstrate respect for one another.

chapter 6

Conclusion & recommendations

Primary caregiving

The parents and teachers involved in my research had a good understanding of primary caregiving principles and expressed their unanimous support for the practice at the case study centre. A team approach to primary caregiving meant the practice did not translate into an exclusive relationship between one teacher and one child, nor was it reliant on the primary caregiver having to always be available to the child. On the contrary, all teachers shared reciprocal relationships with all children with a deeper level of understanding being evident with teachers and the children in their primary care group.

Children would revisit their primary caregiver from time to time and were comfortable when their caregiver was close by. Children were also happy to wait for their turn when needed because teachers were able to communicate through the use of language and gesture that they were aware of them and that they would be next.

Through peaceful observation teachers were able to interpret infants' body language, cues and gestures. Caregivers used a sequential, predictable pattern of body language as invitation to engage. They used language as invitation and explanation with children and also to explain carefully what they were doing and why. Teachers responded to the child's pace and slowed their reactions and interactions accordingly. They also took breaks according to the individual needs and rhythms of the children as opposed to working by the clock.

Free movement

Free movement principles were understood by both parents and teachers at the case study centre. Not all parents were following free movement guidelines at home and some parents were propping their child to sit or restraining them in a high chair. Because of these differing practices between home and centre the teachers were flexible and would sometimes over-ride the guidelines set out by Pikler (1994) making exceptions when children had become used to being sat up if they became frustrated lying down.

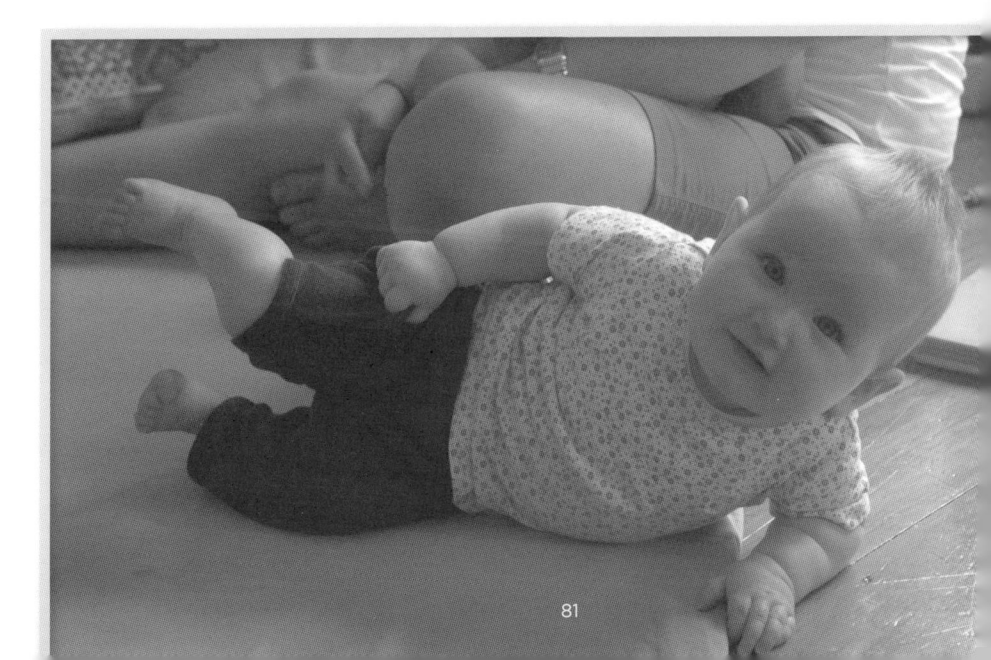

In this way, respect for the child was paramount. In other words, if a child was upset lying down and was not familiar with this practice at home then teachers would sit him up out of respect for parent and child's wishes. This finding highlighted the fundamental difference between the orphanage where the free movement philosophy was used and the case study centre. The children in the case study centre share their time between two different environments where the beliefs and practices might be quite different, as opposed to the consistent environment of an orphanage. This finding is also in alignment with the two principles on which our curriculum Te Whāriki is based: relationships; and family and community.

This research has identified for me the differences between adopting and adapting a philosophy. Adopting the free movement philosophy would involve strictly practising the principles of free movement. Whereas adaptation, as happened in the case study centre, involves taking the ideas from a philosophy and weaving them into the cultural context and curriculum framework within which the centre operates. This results in a more flexible approach to practising these principles.

Another finding regarding free movement was that teachers supported infants rather than intervening. They had a high level of trust in each infant's ability to solve his or her own problems and would allow them the privilege of space and time to do this without intervention. This high level of trust was enabled by the teachers' intimate knowledge of each child, which in turn was developed through peaceful observation.

Future research

Further enquiry into the benefits or otherwise of practising free movement would be beneficial. The research available hails from Pikler's seminal research in an orphanage in Hungary. As this is an entirely different setting to an early childhood centre in New Zealand it would be valuable to investigate the efficacy and relevance of adopting free-movement practices, particularly the idea of unassisted motor development, into early childhood settings in New Zealand. Longitudinal research would be ideal to fully understand the benefits or otherwise of practising free movement, particularly natural motor progression, with infants in early childhood settings.

Respect

My findings indicated that respect was at the heart of the philosophy and practices observed at the case study centre – with respect for children's confidence and competence evident throughout all aspects of the centre programme. Teachers invited children to engage with them and no action would be initiated for or with a child without his or her agreement. This agreement was demonstrated through cues and gestures, to which the teachers were all highly attuned.

Teachers were unhurried in their approach to time and slowed their pace to match the individual rhythms and competencies of each child. They offered children choices in their care and education and waited for the child's response each time. Break times were not observed by the clock but rather were taken at times which seemed convenient to the children and other teachers in the environment.

I have argued that in the use of these practices, teachers displayed an ethic of care and through peaceful observation were able to interpret the actual needs and wants of infants - as opposed to their own perceptions of infants' needs and wants. Teachers would offer support to infants by being close by and observant rather than intervening unnecessarily.

Teachers demonstrated the idea that for infants *care is education and education is care* by maximising the time and attention they paid to routine care times. These were seen as times when a trusting and reciprocal relationship could be built with each child in the understanding that as children are cared for, they learn to care for others. Respect for children's confidence and competence in the case study centre meant inviting children to engage, slowing to the individual child's pace, offering choices, working as a team, paying close attention, and providing support rather than intervention.

Implications and recommendations for policy makers

The implications and recommendations for policy makers are as follows:

- During the time I was observing in the nursery the ratio of infants to teachers was never greater than 1:4. Most often it was 1:3 and often 1:2 or 1:1. It is possible that in order to create and maintain the conditions necessary for this type of respectful practice the required ratio of teachers to children will need to be better than the current minimum standard of 1:5 set out in the New Zealand Early Childhood Education regulations.

- Practical recommendations for creating a peaceful environment and a curriculum based on respect for infants and toddlers would be useful to the sector. The following section presents some practitioner-oriented recommendations that draw on both the findings of this study and literature accessed in the course of this research.

Practical recommendations for teachers

Primary caregiving

The primary caregiver-child relationship is not an exclusive relationship and nor is it a replacement for parents. On the contrary, primary caregiving involves a team approach and for a primary caregiving system to be effective it must be understood and supported by all members of the teaching team and all families who attend the centre. What needs to be understood is that an infant needs to form a strong relationship with at least one other person in the environment and the formation of that relationship is reliant on continuity and trust. For infants, care and education are inseparable because valuable learning is taking place during routine care times and this learning is hindered if the child does not have a strong reciprocal and consistent relationship with the person who is caring for them (Kovach & Da Ros-Vosales, 2008; Lally, 1995). In being cared for, the infant is learning to care for others. This is essentially the basis for a shared sense of humanity which will enable the infant to form and maintain relationships throughout his or her life (Greenspan & Shanker, 2002).

Practical recommendations for teachers

Unhurried time

Time is an essential issue for busy teachers in early childhood centres. In order to give infants unhurried time, teachers have to make a commitment to slow down and be emotionally present when they are interacting with infants. This valuable, uninterrupted, quality time and attention indicates to the child that he is valued which, in turn, enhances his developing self-esteem. This implies that as a team member, one needs to be considerate, thoughtful and aware of the interactions occurring and how one might enhance them by providing space, time, resources, and not interruptions.

Practical recommendations for teachers

Support not intervention

Infants are capable of solving their own problems and having opinions. As the responsible adult we can be tempted to rush in and 'save' the child when he or she looks challenged. These are the moments we need to really challenge our own understanding of what it means to be a teacher in early childhood. Being close by and supportive but allowing an infant the space and time to learn for herself will prove more valuable to that child than 'helping' her by intervening in her learning.

Practical recommendations for teachers

Peaceful observation

Sitting quietly and observing the capabilities, development, understanding and characteristics of an infant will teach much of the knowledge required to be an effective teacher for him. Only when we observe peacefully can we truly know a child and begin to understand his body language, cues, gestures and uniqueness. Slow down and take time to simply observe peacefully as a child explores independently as opposed to trying to engage the infant in activity or always talking to the child. Peaceful observation will lead to a deep level of understanding and empathy.

Practical recommendations for teachers

Respect

Respect is the key to relationships. When you show consideration for another person you communicate to them that they are valued. Feeling valued contributes to a sense of trust and self-esteem and is reflected in the individual's ability to form and maintain relationships with others. A culture of respect in your early childhood centre will mean that interactions between teachers and children are respectful and reciprocal. It will mean that teachers in the team show respect for one another and also that teachers and parents communicate and act respectfully.

References & further reading

Anderson, C. (2009). R-E-S-P-E-C-T – What it means to James L Hymes, Jr: *The Educational Forum*, 73, (4), 298 – 305.

Association Pikler-Loczy. (2005). *The origins of free play.* Hungary, Budapest.

Bary, R. (2009). Time. *Yeah Baby! 2009. A collection of articles for teachers and parents of infants and toddlers* (pp. 18-19). Wellington: Childspace Early Childhood Institute.

Bary, R., Deans, C., Charlton, M., Hullett, H., Martin, F., Martin, L., Moana, P., Waugh, O., Jordan, B., & Scrivens, C. (2009). Paying it forward: COI dissemination. *Generating waves: innovation in early childhood education.* (pp. 21 – 29). Wellington: NZCER Press.

Bernhardt, J.L. (2000). A primary caregiving system for infants and toddlers: Best for everyone involved. *Young Children*, 55(2), 74 – 80.

Brownlee, P. (2008). *Dance with me in the heart: The adults guide to great infant – parent partnerships.* Auckland: Playcentre Publications.

Brownlee, P. (2009). Ego and the baby, or why your colleagues huff and puff when you trust infants. *Yeah Baby 2009! A collection of articles for teachers and parents of infants and toddlers.* (pp. 4-5). Wellington: Childspace Early Childhood Institute.

Brumbaugh, E. (2008). DAP in ECE: Respect. *Kappa Delta Pi Record.* 44 (4), 70 – 175.

Cairns-Cowan, N. & McBride, B. (2010). *In what ways does free movement impact on the social and emotional development of children?* Wellington: Childspace Early Childhood Institute.

Cheshire, N. (2007). The 3 R's: Gateway to Infant and Toddler learning. *Dimensions of Early Childhood.* 35, (3), 36–38.

Christie, T. (2010). *Practising with respect: What does that mean for teachers working with infants?* Unpublished master's thesis, Victoria University of Wellington College of Education, Wellington, New Zealand.

Da Ros, D. & Wong, A. (1996). The Art of being Fully in the Present with Young Children. *Early Childhood Education Journal*, 23(4) 215-216.

Dahlberg, G. & Moss, P. (2005). What Ethics? In G. Dahlberg & P. Moss (Eds.), *Ethics and Politics in Early Childhood Education* (pp. 64-85). London: Routledge.

Dalli, C., Kibble, N., Carins-Cowan, N., Corrigan, J. & McBride, B. (2009). Reflecting on primary caregiving through action research: The centre of innovation experience at Childspace Ngaio Infants and Toddlers centre. *The First Years: Nga Tau Tautahi. NZ Journal of Infant and Toddler Education.* 11 (2), 38 – 45.

Dalli, C. & Kibble, N. (2010). Peaceful caregiving as curriculum: Insights on primary caregiving from action research. *Dispersing Waves: Innovation in Early Childhood Education.* (pp. 27-34). Wellington: NZCER Press.

Dalli, C. (2000). Starting childcare: What young children learn about relating to adults in the first weeks of starting childcare. *Early Childhood Research and Practice,* 2 (2). Available at http://ecrp.uiuc.edu/v2n2/dalli.html.

David, M., & Appell, G. (2001) Loczy: *An unusual approach to mothering.* Budapest: Association Pikler Loczy for Young Children.

Elfer, P., Goldschmied, E., & Selleck, D. (2003) *Key persons in the nursery: Building relationships for quality provision.* London: Fulton Publishers.

Falkner, A. (2009). You can't play peek-a-boo on your tummy. *The First Years: Nga Tau Tautahi. NZ Journal of Infant and Toddler Education.* 11 (2) 13–17.

Gerber, M. (1979). *The RIE manual for parents and professionals.* Los Angeles: Resources for Infant Educarers (RIE).

Gerber, M. (1984). Caring for infants with respect: The RIE approach. *Zero to Three,* 4(4), 1-3.

Gerber, M. (1998, and reprinted 2002). *Dear parent: Caring for infants with respect.* (2nd Ed.). Edited by J. Weaver. Los Angeles: Resource for Infant Educarers.

Gerber, M., & Johnson, A. (1998). *Your self confident baby: How to encourage your child's natural abilities – from the very start.* New York: Wiley.

Goffin, S. (1990). How well do we respect the children in our care? *The Education Digest* 55(8), 37-40.

Goldstein, L. (1998). More than gentle smiles and warm hugs: Applying the ethic of care to early childhood education. *Journal of Research in Childhood Education.* 12, (2), 244 – 256.

Gonzalez-Mena, J. (2007). What to do for a fussy baby: A problem solving approach. *Young Children,* 62 (5), 20 – 25.

Gonzalez-Mena, J., & Widmeyer Eyer, D. (2007). *Infants, toddlers and caregivers: A curriculum of respectful, responsive care and education* (7th ed.). Boston: McGraw-Hill Higher Education.

Gonzalez-Mena, J. (2009). How to get infants and toddlers to co-operate: A simple but effective approach. *Yeah Baby! 2009. A collection of articles for teachers and parents of infants and toddlers.* Wellington: Childspace Early Childhood Institute.

Greenman, J., & Stonehouse, A. (1997). *Prime times: A handbook for excellence in infant and toddler programs.* Melbourne, Vic., Australia: Longman.

Greenspan, S., & Shanker, S. (2002). *Towards a psychology of global interdependency: A framework for international collaboration.* Bethesda MD: Interdisciplinary Council on Developmental and Learning Disorders.

Hammond, R. (2009). *Respecting babies: A new look at Magda Gerber's RIE approach.* Zero to Three: Washington DC.

Hannaford, C. (2005). *Smart moves: Why learning is not all in your head.* (2nd Ed). Salt Lake City, UT: Great River Books.

Hutchins, T., & Sims, M. (1999). *Program planning for infants and toddlers: An Ecological approach.* Sydney, NSW, Australia: Prentice Hall.

Johnson, J. (2007). *Journey through RIE: My experiences incorporating the RIE Philosophy into a traditional childcare setting.* Fitchburg: Fitchburg State College.

Kibble, N. (2009). Re-thinking infant play spaces. *Yeah Baby 2009! A collection of articles for teachers and parents of infants and toddlers* (pp. 22-23). Wellington: Childspace Early Childhood Institute.

Kibble, N., Cairns-Cowan, N., McBride, B., Corrigan, J., Dalli, C. (2009). *Primary caregiving: a way of being.* Retrieved February 23, 2010, from http://www.educate.ece.govt.nz/EducateHome/Programmes/CentresOfInnovation/RoundFour/-/media/Educate/Files/Reference%20Downloads/documents%20for%20upload/ChildspaceCOI.pdf.

Kibble, N., Cairns-Cowan, N., McBride, B., Corrigan, J., Dalli, C. (2010). Primary Caregiving: It's a team approach. *Yeah Baby 2010! A collection of articles for teachers and parents of infants and toddlers* (pp. 5-9). Wellington: Childspace Early Childhood Institute.

Kovach, B., & Da Ros, D. (1998). Respectful, individual, and responsive caring for infants: the key to successful care in group settings. *Young Children* 53(3), 61-74.

Kovach, B., & Da Ros – Voseles, D. (2008) *Being with babies: Understanding and responding to the infants in your care.* Silver Spring, MD: Gryphon House.

Lally, J.R. (1995). The impact of child care policies and practices on infant/toddler identity formation. *Young children* 51(1), 58-67.

Leon-Weil & Hewitt (2008). Trust as a teaching skill. *Young Children* September 2008. (pp. 24 – 26).

Meade, A (Ed.) (2010) *Dispersing waves: Innovation in early childhood education.* Wellington: NZCER Press.

Miller, R. & Pedro, J. (2006). Creating Respectful Classroom Environments. *Early Childhood Education Journal.* 33 (5). 293 – 299.

Ministry of Education (1996). *Te Whāriki: He whariki matauranga mo nga mokopuna o Aotearoa: Early Childhood Curriculum.* Wellington: Ministry of Education.

Ministry of Education. (2007). *Education Counts* website. Retrieved June 5, 2008 from www.educationcounts.govt.nz.

Ministry of Education (2009). *Annual ECE Summary Report 2009.* Retrieved June 4, 2010, from http://www.educationcounts.govt.nz/statistics/ece/55413/licensed-services-and-licence-exempt-groups/65543.

Money, R. (Ed). (2006). *Unfolding of infants' natural gross motor development.* Los Angeles: Resources for Infant Educarers.

Noddings, N. (1984). *Caring.* Berkeley, CA: University of California Press.

Petrie, S., & Owen, S. (2005). *Authentic relationships in Group Care for Infants and Toddlers – Resources for Infant Educarers (RIE) Principles into practice.* Philadelphia: Jessica Kingsley Publishers.

Pikler, E. (1971) Learning of motor skills on the basis of self-induced movements. In J. Hellmuth (ed) *Exceptional Infant: Studies in Abnormalities Vol. 2.* New York and London: Bruner / Mazel and Butterworth.

Pikler, E. (1994) Peaceful babies – contented mothers. In M.E. Roche (ed) *Sensory Awareness Bulletin 14,* Muir Beach, CA: Sensory Awareness foundation.

Porter, P (2003). *Social relationships of infants in daycare.* http://www.educarer.com/current-article-relationships.htm Accessed 19 February 2008.

Rockel, J. (2002). *Teachers and parents understandings of primary care for infants in early childhood centres within a New Zealand context.* : Unpublished master's thesis, Massey University, Palmerston North, New Zealand.

Rockel, J. (2003). "Someone is going to take the place of Mum and Dad and understand": Teachers' and parents' perceptions of primary care for infants in early childhood centres. *New Zealand Research in Early Childhood,* volume 6, 113-126.

Rogoff, B. (2003). *The cultural nature of human development.* New York: Oxford University Press.

Saracho, O. & Spodek, B. (2003). Recent Trends and Innovations in the Early Childhood Education Curriculum. *Early Child Development and Care,* 173(2-3), 175-183.

Sensory Awareness Foundation (1994). Emmi Pikler 1902 – 1984. *Sensory Awareness Bulletin,* 14, 1-48.

Shonkhoff, J., & Phillips, D. (Eds.). (2000). *From neurons to neighborhoods.* Washington, DC: National Academy Press.

Slaveron, M., Arney, F., & Scott, D. (2006). Sowing the seeds of innovation: Ideas for child and family services. *Family Matters,* 73, 38-45.

Smith, A. (2007). Children's rights and early childhood education: Links to theory and advocacy. *Australian Journal of Early Childhood,* 32(3), 1-8.

Te One, S. (2010). *Supporting children's rights.* The Space, 19, 8.

Te One. S. (2008). *Children's perceptions of their rights in a New Zealand Kindergarten.* Paper presented at the NZARE Annual Conference, Palmerston North, New Zealand.

Tharp, R.G., & Gallimore, R. (1988). *Rousing minds to life: Teaching, learning, and schooling in social context.* New York: Cambridge University Press.

Theilheimer, R. (2006). Molding to the children: Primary caregiving and continuity of care. *Zero to Three,* 26 (3), 50-54.

Triulzi, M. (2008). *Do the Pikler and RIE methods promote infant-parent attachment?* Unpublished master's thesis, Smith College School for Social Work, Northampton, Massachusetts.

Tronto, J. (1993). *Moral boundaries: A political argument for an ethic of care.* New York: Routledge.

United Nations Committee on the Rights of the Child. (2003). *Concluding observations of the Committee on the Rights of the Child: New Zealand,* 34th session. UN Doc CRC/C/15/Add.216, 3 October, Geneva

Publications available from Childpsace Early Childhood Institute

Peaceful Caregiving as Curriculum DVD: a guide to respectful care practices...

This interactive DVD allows you to see a 'peaceful caregiving curriculum' in practice. This guide to respectful care practices has been designed so you are able to use it in a variety of ways providing a versatile, reflective resource. It will give teachers and parents a unique insight into how the work of Emmi Pikler & Magda Gerber has inspired our team to provide a peaceful approach for the infants and toddlers in their care.

Pennie Brownlee:
Dance with me in the Heart: the adults' guide to great infant-parent partnerships

Pennie has done it again. A timeless, brilliant, frank and respectful guide for anyone who cares for infants. An absolute must for your parenting library.

This is an easy yet thoroughly engaging read, with simple steps for care and respect, making it easy to find your footing as you coordinate the first steps of your relationship as dance partners.

Yeah Baby! 2009 & Yeah Baby! 2010: collections of articles

These inspirational collections of articles were put together to mark our two infant & toddler conferences – *Yeah Baby! 2009 & Yeah Baby! 2010*.

If your vision is to create an atmosphere of awe and wonder for babies then this collection is a must for your library.

Yeah Baby! 2011: CD-ROM

This CD-ROM will be a valuable addition to any teaching library. There are more than fifty articles by various authors specific to learning and teaching with infants and toddlers.

To order products or obtain a copy of our free catalogue please contact us:

Childspace
Early Childhood Institute

45 Helston Road, Johnsonville,
Wellington 6037, New Zealand.
Phone: **(+64 4) 461 7076** • Fax: **(+64 4) 478 3986**
www.childspace.co.nz

95